"YOU HAVE TO LAUGH TO KEEP FROM CRYING!"

Cherron Covington

OWN YOUR OWN PUBLISHING, LLC

"YOU HAVE TO LAUGH TO KEEP FROM CRYING!"

This book is dedicated to the Lord. He helped me keep my sanity at a time when I really thought I was losing it for sure this time. To my grandma, Elsie, looking down on me from heaven, wishing the best for me always. Thanks also goes to all those <u>real</u> friends of mine who helped me pull myself out of a black hole I thought I would never leave.

PREFACE

This book is about me, but it's not my memoirs. It gets to be boring, after a while with everyone writing about their life, you know.

Yes, I am African American. I was a victim of incest, while living in the projects of Washington, DC. I'm an adult child of an alcoholic (my stepfather was one), statistics tell me. I was emotionally and physically abused by my mother. She had me using her husband's last name from 3rd grade to 12th grade; I used it so long I forgot my real last name. I left her house at 18 pregnant with my oldest daughter. I was sent to Catholic church as a child, so I knew God was above, I asked Him to teach me how to love because I didn't know how, to make me the mommy I wish I had had and I wanted a relationship with my children. Little did I know I was asking Him to break some generational curses. After my first divorce, I had to pay a lawyer to do a name change to go back to using a name that was legally mine all the time. To this day I still don't know why she hates me like she does. At the time of this book, I was the only one who had given her grandchildren and they don't mean a thing to her. My grandma Elsie, my mother's mother, was my world. She taught me that I didn't have to become a product of my environment. She showed me that no matter what, keep your head up and you can do anything you want. She never said much but when she did, it made me think. She died two months after I moved to Atlanta in 1986. The last thing she said to me before she got worse (she died of cancer of the liver) was, "some of Pandora's boxes are better left unopened". At the time I didn't understand what she meant. I believe she told me that because I had been so insistent on meeting the man, I was told was my father.

I got married the first time too young. I tried to have a marriage like the ones I grew up watching on TV. I soon realized I was not June Cleaver, Daddy didn't want room made for him and this father didn't know what was best for him, let alone me and our daughters. The second time was to someone who was looking for a way out of his present situation. I'm what I call a magnet for the wrong type of men.

I've finally learned to weed them out, so I spend a lot of time alone trying to keep me busy with the children and my business. Therapy helped me get rid of some of the ghosts that haunted me and made me realize that it was okay to be me.

I've raised my two oldest daughters trying to find out who I was. I tried to set a good example, while helping them find out who they were. I've taken them through some very hard times, I now have a third daughter who I hope won't see as hard a time as her sisters did.

See I learned parenting wasn't something you could turn on and off. Having a biological mother and a stepmother, who both let me know I was a thorn in their side. A biological father who was still apologizing to his wife for my coming about. A stepfather who didn't care about anyone, not even himself. These people who should have been the ones who molded me into the type of person who would give back, made me want to be the best mommy I could be. I know God lead me to Him and I'm glad I answered the call.

> "When my father and my mother forsake me,
> Then the Lord will take care of me." (Psalm 27:10)

He became the parents I wish I had had. He finished raising me and taught me the ways of my brother Jesus. I thank Him for that every day.

No matter what, I have never given up or done something that would make me hate myself later. Through it all the Lord never let me down. He held me and helped me through the worst of times. I began to pray Psalm 91 over me and my family daily. I've had a lot of situations and God always pulled me back from the gates of hell when they began to open to suck me in. I've been in God's University of Hard Knocks, got a master's degree, I told Him I didn't want a doctorate degree. God gave me what I asked Him for, I am the mommy I wish I had had, I love my babies unconditionally and free of charge, as God loves me and I have a relationship with my daughters and it's AMAZING.

STRESSED

It all started Fall of 1989. I had my tubes untied to
have another child because it was a possibility of
me having to have a hysterectomy. August 1990 I
was with child and had just separated from my
husband during the summer, the stress of it all
caused me to go into labor early. Being only 26
weeks at the time, the labor was halted. I was put
on medication and put on bedrest, thus making me
unable to return to work. The medication, called
"brethene", stops the contractions and labor all
together. You still must be careful, keeping still
most of the time. The brethene had side effects that
scared me often. My heart would race, I would get
the shakes really bad. I guess that would make you
stay home because outside you would look like
maybe you had some kind of disability or a habit of
some kind. At the time, I was working through a
temporary service. I would call my agency daily
and ask if there were any assignments available for
me, to no avail. Sometimes I would leave the house
and just ride the bus, reading my Bible. I didn't
really have a home church at that time but knew I
needed one desperately. Often times I would get off
the bus and go to the library. I walked slow as if
my stomach might fall off me if I rocked it too
much. Sometimes I had to laugh at myself with
some of my silliness.

By November my rent was behind, and I had to go
apply for Public Assistance. That added to the
stress because I had two ex-husbands, who weren't
sending me any money.

When it dawned on me to apply for unemployment it was denied because my doctor said I could not go back to work until after the baby was born. After going into premature labor, I ran into an ex-coworker and friend. We had lunch and caught up on what was going on with each other. It was at this time I asked him if he would be my labor coach, he was pleased I asked. As time went on, he would come over and talk to my baby in Arabic in the womb to calm her down. I believe that's why she picks up foreign languages so quickly. I realized it was important to keep a positive attitude and positive people around during my pregnancy. Unborn babies may reflect what they picked up during those nine months inside the womb.

One day while walking back to my apartment, I met her, Melissa, at least that's what she told me her name was. She lived upstairs over my apartment with her three sons. I had seen my girls playing with some boys before, I figured they must have been hers. She invited me upstairs a couple times, she seemed pleasant and "harmless". Looks can be deceiving I learned.

My baby girl was born the beginning of December, as an emergency C-section. I never felt so alone that afternoon. My so-called labor coach had come by earlier and said he would be back. I told him I knew for sure I would be going in that day (I had 6 false alarms by this time). Well by midnight he had not returned so I had to walk to a neighbors to call an ambulance to come and get me. I was in labor until noon the next day. When they tried to induce labor my baby's heart rate dropped to "0". All kinds of awful thoughts ran through my head. I thought I might lose my baby. Then I looked up at the TV and Kenneth Copeland was on. I turned up the TV and at that time very moment he was saying, "Remember God is always with you, with Him you are never alone". At that moment I said thank you to Kenneth Copeland and to God. I prayed and suddenly felt everything was going to be okay. I relaxed and the staff was able to stabilize me and my baby. By the time we settled down my doctor had arrived and informed me that they would have to do a C-section. A whole new experience for me because my first two were born naturally with no problems. My doctor and the whole staff in labor and delivery at Crawford Long Hospital were wonderful. They talked to me and kept me relaxed and let me know everything that was happening as it occurred. Jocelyn Olivia (Joc, pronounced Josh) was born at 12:59pm, cold and she seemed mad that she was going to miss lunch. We ate well daily; lunch was always at 1:00pm.

I went home three days later, only to be reminded that I was due in court for eviction and Christmas was coming. It was hard getting around after having a C-section, but I had business to attend to. I put on a girdle and wrapped up really good to go outside. By this time my mother-in-law had come to town to help me with her new granddaughter and my other two daughters. In court I was told to pay the balance owed or move out by December 29th. After I left the courthouse, I had to go to the

Salvation Army. I had put myself on their list for Christmas, just in-case. I'm glad I did, we didn't hear from my oldest children's father or either side of the family to see if the girls needed anything; but they still had Christmas. I was able to pick out some very nice things for each girl, even the new baby. I caught a cab home and slept the rest of the day putting what the court said aside so that I could allow my daughters to enjoy Christmas, which was the following week. Christmas day, one of Melissa's sons knocked on the door and said his mother said come upstairs. So, I picked up my baby and went upstairs to see what she wanted. When I went up, she had company, so I said I couldn't stay long. I was introduced to two men; one was to later become her boyfriend. I stayed for a short time and then went back downstairs.

The following day I started going upstairs regularly, I guess I just wanted some company or someone to talk to. With all I had been through anybody being nice would have fit the bill. Melissa told me at that time she was on vacation but that in January, she was being put on medical leave because she had to have some tests run. She stated that her health hadn't been that good in the last few months. We were just talking, and I mentioned that I had to move out of the apartment because I couldn't come up with the rent money. Well Melissa said, "Why don't you and the girls come stay up here. I have a third bedroom that's not really being used, you could move your bed up here and put it in there". I said,

"I can't do that; you don't even know me". That's when she said, "If you stay here the girls can stay at the same school, at least until the end of the school term". She hit me below the belt. She knew moving the girls was a concern of mine. I said I would think about it and let her know. I didn't have enough time to go on a three day fast. I really didn't want to move the girls from the school they were attending; we had only been in the complex since August and the second report period was just starting. I went downstairs with a big decision to make.

LOOKING FOR AN ANSWER

I fell asleep that night with a lot on my mind. I prayed and asked God to please tell me what to do.

You know, sometimes we can ask the Lord what to do in a situation but want our answer rushed. If we don't pay attention and wait to hear from Him, we think He's answered because it might be what we want to hear at the time. I learned this the hard way to wait for Him to answer me with his own words. Now when I pray, I say, "Lord, could you give me the message loud, because I don't want to miss it". I say this because I really thought that the Lord had sent her to me. Boy! were my lines of communication crossed.

I moved upstairs December 30. I took as much upstairs as I could, the rest I put in storage. The girls and I shared the room; my nightmare begins. Things started out okay. We got along well, her boys and my girls became very attached to each other. Melissa and I shared a lot of things. I paid my half of everything, and bought the food, as I received food stamps monthly.

It's May, my new baby is five months old, and school is about to end for my older girls. I realized I bought most of the food and cooked most of the time. I would, every now and then, smoke some marijuana with Melissa. She and her friends liked when I smoked, because I would get the "munchies" and just start cooking; I would cook so much that she would have to tell me to stop cooking. One particular day, she came in the kitchen and gave me a lit "joint", I took a few puffs off, passed it back and she left the kitchen. I soon started feeling something was not right, I had a feeling I had never had before. I went in the living room to sit down and told my oldest daughter to bring me some ice, I put it on the back of my neck, but it was not helping. I started praying, asking God to please help me with this situation, to stop it, whatever it was that was happening; I promised Him I would never touch marijuana again if He fixed this situation. I planned to keep this vow I made to Him, because I wanted to make sure I was the person raising my children. I began to calm down, mentally, my breathing slowed, and my head stopped swimming. I realized the joint must have been laced with something. I begin to think about what I had been experiencing was my soul leaving me, understanding why a "crack high" is referred to as being "beamed up". I also realized that is why the first crack high can never be recaptured, as you only have one soul.

After a while, I felt better and relieved, I thanked God and tried NOT to think about what could have happened to my daughters if God had not snatched me back from the gates of hell as they opened to pull me in. When she came back out of her room, I think she looked somewhat surprised that I was not high and asking for more. I knew then I better hurry and get me and my children away from this situation.

Melissa was always introducing me to a new guy. I got to where I stayed in my room a lot or left when she had company. I guess she felt since she was seeing someone I should also. I later found out she sold and smoked marijuana, this didn't go over well with me at all. I started thinking its time to move. I also wondered why she hadn't said anything else about her poor health. I noticed she had two other men in her life that she had come over regularly also. I began to wonder if she really worked at all. It was almost tax time and I had decided to move with my income tax check. I knew with the new "Rapid Refund" system I would have my refund back in three to five days. So, whenever we went out, when she could get one of her men's cars, I would look for rental properties. I wanted to move into a house with the girls. I was getting unemployment by this time, along with the check from Public Assistance and food stamps. My caseworker had told me I only had to report "earned income" she had me believing that my unemployment didn't have to be reported.

One day while we were out, she noticed me writing down some things and asked me what was I doing. I told her I was looking for a house for me and the girls. She was silent for a moment then said she was looking for a house also. She said she needed at least five bedrooms. I asked her what she needed all that space for, and she said that she and the boys had talked it over and they didn't want the girls and I to leave. She wanted us to move into a house together. I told her that was nice, but that I was sure that she and the boys were tired of us by now. I told her I felt that the girls and I were in the way, especially with her and Eric getting as close as they were day-to-day. She told me that until he was ready to fully commit to her she didn't want to take a chance on depending on him later on down the road.

Here I am still wearing "blinders". Then she said she needed to confide in me and what she was about to say, I was to tell no one, not even her sisters. She proceeded to tell me she had incurable cancer. I was shocked and felt sorry for her, I believed her because she looked sickly all the time. I really felt for her boys. She said she felt better with me around with the boys, because she would be starting treatment soon. I told her I would think about it. She said she would soon be undergoing a lot of tests and maybe even chemotherapy. Melissa said she had no one else to keep the boys. I know, I know, you may be wondering why I was not asking the Lord to help me on this one and why would He let me be suckered into this situation ---- right. Well, when you're not in tune to the word of the Lord, not reading His word like you should, you miss out on things He may be trying to tell you. I was still reading my bible, but not picking up and taking in the word like I should have. I was still in the crawling stage of my faith and learning. Let's go on shall we.

DECISIONS, DECISIONS

That night I hardly slept; a lot of things ran through my mind. I wanted to help her because she had helped me, but at the same time I was ready for my own space. Weighing my pros and cons, it was like this ---- I still had no job, a possible interview, possibly a job, but I had to get it first. My baby was just three months old and I really was not in a position to foot all the bills at this time. Also, I had no babysitter lined up yet. If I did get the job, at least Melissa could baby-sit for me, she loved my baby, more than I knew.

The next day, I told Melissa I would stay until we knew she was on the road to recovery. I figured I could save some money and get me a car as well. So together we started looking for a big enough house for all of us. She found one and inquired about it but never got a call back.

Two weeks later I found a house while looking through the Sunday paper. I went and looked at it and when I saw it, I knew Melissa and the kids would like it. It was huge and had a basement (which would later become my bedroom). When Melissa called from her boyfriend's house, I told her to go look at the house and tell me what she thought. We set up time to go look at the house, but I didn't get to go. I assumed we'd look at the house together and we'd both sign the lease. Boy! was I wrong -- again. She and her boyfriend looked at it, to make the Realtor think that the two of them and her three boys were the only ones moving in and living there. (I found this out after I had given her my half of the $1500 down payment). When we sat down and decided we'd take the house after looking at the monthly estimated expenses, I wasn't comfortable with the situation, but I didn't know why. When I picked up my income tax check, I started thinking why don't I just take an apartment with the girls and make the best of it, a job will come, "oh yea of little faith", huh. I see now that the strength of my faith was seriously weak. I had a job interview, but still it was not guaranteed. So, I was still stuck, I felt like I was between a rock and a hard place. I Just didn't want to go through the possibility of money running out again before a job came along. Didn't want to be evicted anymore, wanted things to be easy for a while. I asked her again if the Realtor knew eight of us were going to be living in the house and she said yes. I gave her $745 in cash (my fault, should have been a money order) for my half to move in. When she came home with the lease the next day it was just her name on it and her three boys. Only five people were to occupy the house, well I was out of $745 and wondering what was going to happen next. Moving day was awful, she fussed at everybody, she was only interested in getting her things moved. When we got to the house, I had my bed put downstairs. I made my room in the basement. It had a woodburning stove, a full bathroom, and a door so I could enter the house from outside, without having to come through the upstairs. Then I got all my other things out of storage and moved them into the house. She didn't seem to like it, but I didn't let it bother me. She would often say why don't you share the room with the girls. I let her know I was not going to pay half of everything and not have my own room, she had her own room. I began to realize she wanted her friends and family thinking she was doing me a big favor by helping me out. She wanted it to look like she was footing all the expenses alone; like I had no income and she was paying all the bills. She was really obsessed with my baby daughter. She always wanted a little girl, claimed she had lost one the year before. I began to wonder if that was the reason, she wanted me to stay, so that she could share my baby. We moved March 2, 1991 and I went to work for a law firm March 11, 1991. Melissa said she would keep the baby and I paid her $100 every two weeks. I got my last unemployment check March 18, 1991. I put the check stub in the trash can by my bed. I knew that if you didn't mail in a stub, you wouldn't receive a check. I stopped receiving unemployment leaving about $2,400 in my account when I returned to the working world. I didn't inform unemployment that I was working, Big Mistake. I just went on my assumption they would close my claim once the claims stopped being mailed in. I kept receiving the public assistance for a month because I needed the Medicaid for myself and my daughters. If I had stopped the check right away, the baby was the only one who would have been eligible for Medicaid, the two big girls were too old, they couldn't be over five.

EYE OPENERS

April 8th, I bought a car, that was one of the stipulations of my getting the job, that I have my own transportation. Sometimes I had to go to the different county courthouses to pick up different lists of upcoming cases. Now things are really starting to heat at home. I believe Melissa was getting jealous of my getting back on my feet. From my room in the basement, I would hear her talking to her boyfriend, since her room was over my head. She would say little things to her boyfriend about her not needing me to help her pay her bills; and how I could get out if I didn't like what was going on there. I learned around the beginning of April she was still selling marijuana and thinking about getting into selling cocaine. I knew then it was truly time to go. I figured this was probably how she was paying her half of the bills. So, my goal, very, very short term, was to get out, quickly. Soon it got to where I didn't want to leave my baby with her. The baby started acting as though she didn't want to stay either. She cried often, especially when I left in the morning. I started having bad vibes. She was also taking my baby to Columbus, Georgia to her boyfriend's mother's house. This was a four-hour ride away and I didn't like that at all.

My older daughters were doing very well in school. They had no idea what was going on around them. I had noticed that Melissa never showed her sons any kind of affection at all. The boys noticed me kissing my daughters "good night" every night and they too started coming to me for a good night kiss.

I mentioned she had two sisters, both older than her and both in bad shape. One was an alcoholic and the other a drug addict. They never did it at the house, but you could tell they were high whenever they would come over. They would come over with their boyfriends and Melissa would cook all this food for them. They'd also bring their alcohol with them too. I was no "saint", but there comes a time when you must draw the line for yourself. You stop and take a good look at yourself and where you are. How far do I want to reach up? I just didn't care for some of the things they were doing. Always tried to keep myself and my daughters away from negative environments. I start noticing the only people she associated with were people who weren't doing as well as she was. It wasn't like she was doing that great, she just made it seem like it. She needed to feel as if she was better than they were. Melissa didn't like anyone around she couldn't impress. She didn't like me having company at all. She knew that the people I knew had more than she had then or would ever have. She had people she dealt with thinking she was buying the house. She also had them thinking she was helping poor Cherron, since she was soooooooooooooooooooooooooooooooooo unfortunate.

MAKING A MOVE

In May Melissa got real sick, I don't know why, she didn't really have cancer, I later came to learn. She was often weak and told me it was from the medicine she was taking. Oh, by the way, she told me she had finally started taking chemotherapy ---- yeah, right. I took this opportunity to change baby-sitters, using her sickness as an excuse.

While at work this one day, I decided to call her office, or so I thought, to see if she really worked there, or even if the place existed. She was supposed to have worked for this insurance company as the supervisor in accounting. I called the company only to find out there was no such office at the location where she said she was based. So, I then called the main office to see if she was listed as an employee, they didn't know who I was talking about. This made me really feel much better about having my baby with someone else. I began looking for an apartment in the area where my girls were in school so they could remain there. They were doing so well I didn't want to interrupt that. I didn't say anything to Melissa, but I guessed she could feel the distance between us getting wider.

One day after I had gotten home from work, a lady knocked on the door. When Melissa opened the door, she told Melissa she was there for the rent. Melissa swore it had been mailed and produced an envelope from her room. She claimed that the receipts were in there. She started talking and hollering so loud that she scared the lady and she left.
I knew I had given her my half, but I always gave it to her in cash. She went back to her room and told Eric what had happened. To calm her down they left to go for a ride. I went downstairs to get my shampoo to wash my hair and couldn't find it. I knew where to look. I went to Melissa's room and got it out of her bathroom. On my way out, I spotted the envelope; yes, my curiosity got the best of me and I looked inside. There were two money order receipts all right, but not for the rent, they totaled $150, the rent was $725. I also saw checks and cards in other people's names, wondering why she had these things, and it dawned on me she had stolen them, I knew then I really needed to get out

of there. I started speaking to less and not spending any time in presence when she was home.

When she had company, I would take my daughters and stay in the basement. I had hidden all my important papers so that no one would go in them while I was at work. By May, she started saying little things to my girls that made them feel uncomfortable. She started leaving them out when she cooked or handed out snacks. So, when I knew I had found an apartment (it wasn't going to be ready until June 7th), I would go home, pick them up and go visiting. I fed them out and would return just in time for them to go to bed. It got to the point where her boys were picking on my girls because they resented them being gone all the time. After a while I didn't even want my girls there if they didn't have to be. I kept praying over them while I was away.

Another stipulation of the job at the law firm was that I had to work one Saturday a month. This particular Friday night, I went to bed early because I had to work that
Saturday. Melissa, her sisters and their boyfriends had been making noise and drinking since early evening. Around 3:00am Melissa turned the stereo up real loud. Eric said, "Cherron's sleep, you know she's got to go to work tomorrow". Melissa said, "I don't give a F...., if she doesn't like it, she can get the F..... out. I don't know who that B....... thinks she is, I don't need her". At that, I couldn't leave soon enough. I even begin fearing going to sleep at night. I didn't even want my girls sleeping upstairs. A lot of nights I made them sleep downstairs with me. On the nights they preferred to sleep upstairs I

said a prayer and left them in God's hands. The next day I took the girls to a friend's house so that they wouldn't be with Melissa alone. I didn't trust leaving them there with her while I was gone for a long period of time, anymore.

Memorial Day was coming up, I decided to take my daughters to Lake Lanier for the weekend. I did not want to spend the whole weekend with Melissa and her sisters. We returned late afternoon on Memorial Day. The basement had this huge pool table in it; when we moved in Melissa swore no one would be playing on it. Well all of a sudden, they were all interested in playing pool. They were all in my room playing pool when we got in. I had to put up with this for about three hours. I turned up my television set loud so that I could drown them out and they finally got the message and went back upstairs. When they went upstairs, she started ranting and raving again. Summer and June were approaching fast but not fast enough for me. One day I came home, and no one was there but Eric and Melissa's oldest sister's boyfriend. They were playing pool in my room. I got mad because they didn't even leave when I came in. I was already hot and bothered and couldn't wait to get out of my pantyhose. I felt they should have had the decency to leave so that I could change my clothes. I had to change in the bathroom, I didn't even speak to either one of them, except to ask where my daughters were. Eric told me that Melissa had taken everyone to the store. I left to go pick up the baby and buy her some formula. When I returned the kids were outside playing. I went in through my door and stayed downstairs. After about an hour or so Melissa came downstairs and asked if she could talk with me. All this time she has no idea what I've learned about her and her so called job, nor did she know I'd been looking for a place of my own. She sat at the bottom of the steps and said that Eric told her that I had an attitude when I came in and didn't speak. I told her yes, I did, I wanted to change my clothes and they didn't leave when I came in. I told her I was not obligated to speak to her man or anyone else's, they weren't there to see me. Right then I felt this would be a good opportunity to bring up my moving. I told her that since the weather was changing and they would probably be using the basement more, I thought it best I move. I didn't need any unnecessary problems. I told her I felt the girls and I had worn out our welcome and it was best. I would try to be out by June. Eventually, she started telling my daughters that she didn't cook enough dinner for them since she never knew when they were going to be there to eat. So, they would have to wait until I got home to eat. I still said nothing so that hopefully my daughters would be all right while I was at work. One day Melissa came downstairs to tell me she had found a school in Texas where she could get a trade free of charge. She stated she was thinking about going to Texas, and that this school would put her up in a place, etc. I told her I thought that was nice and good luck to her. I noticed she started trying to be nice, but I didn't know why. In the days that followed, Melissa kept talking about leaving town and flying with her sons, I was wondering "How" she could afford airfare for four people, little did I know. She also kept asking if my baby could spend the day with her and I kept saying no. I told her I didn't want to interrupt the baby's routine with the new sitter.

ON MY OWN

June 7, 1991, moving day for me and my daughters.
I moved out of the house I shared with Melissa and
gave her my half of the rent since I didn't give her
thirty days notice. (Stupid me) Earlier that day I
had the post office put a hold on all <u>my</u> mail. I told
them I would pick it up on Monday, June 10th and
put in my change of address at that time. I moved
everything in one trip. I was glad to be gone.

Monday, June 10th, I picked up my mail from the
post office. I put in a change of address card and
had all my mail forwarded to my new apartment.
When I checked my mail, I noticed I had an
unemployment check, I couldn't figure out why
they might have
sent it other than the fact that they had changed the
format of the checks. I just deposited it in my
savings account and thought no more of it. June
12th, Melissa called me at work. She asked me if I
had had all the mail forwarded because she had not
received her disability check for the week before. I
told her that the only mail I had forwarded was my
own. Then she said she and the boys wanted to see
us and could she bring them over. Me not thinking,
told her it would be all right and gave her my
address. I had nothing against the children and felt
they needed someone they could talk to or someone
they knew would be there if they needed them.
Well as far as I was concerned things were looking
up for me and my family. I was finally doing okay
financially and could exhale for the moment.

June 15th my daughters and I were invited to go to Miami, FL. A good friend of mine was getting married and asked me to be the matron of honor. Never having been to Florida before I said okay. I drove one car with my daughters and one of her sons. Her fiancee was already in Florida. We left Friday night, by Saturday morning we were on the Florida Turnpike and decided to race each other. We got stopped by a state trooper who clocked us each at 125 mph. Yes, we did get tickets but were allowed to keep our driver's license and go on. A ticket was the last thing I needed taking away from my budget but I put it aside for now. This was a happy moment for my friend. Miami was beautiful. All three of my daughters had the best time. We were leaving to go back on Sunday, we stayed in a Hyatt Hotel right off the water. I enjoyed seeing my daughters laugh, which was something they were just starting to do again since we had moved away from Melissa. We got plenty of sun and relaxation. The wedding was Saturday, it went really well, and everyone had a good time. Boy was it hot there. The water was so clear and pretty unlike any I had ever seen. Sunday, I headed back to Georgia. My friend's brother rode back with me since we both had jobs to get back to by Monday. We stopped in Kissimee, Florida and went to an amusement park and rode the monorail to the outside of Disney. I promised my daughters we would come back one day so that they could go in. We got home late Sunday night.

I FEEL SICK

June 27, 1991, my life suddenly started falling apart again. I was laid-off my job. This was also the day

I was to take my daughters to Washington, DC for their summer vacation. They had started going up there to spend time with my maternal aunt. I had already rented the car and decided I would take them anyway. Maybe during the time, I was away something good would fall into my lap. I needed a serious miracle. I would at least save grocery money and utility money for a month or so while they were gone. I was given severance pay and a separation notice for unemployment purposes. I went to Washington and stayed a while since I didn't have to hurry back. I came back July 2nd and remembered I still had at least $2,000 left from my last unemployment claim. I figured I'd use up the old claim and then put in the new claim when I returned. So, I decided to wait a couple of days before I went down to the unemployment office. There was a message on my answering machine from Melissa when I returned home. She asked if my baby could spend the day with her and her boys. With the way I felt about her I wouldn't dare let my baby stay with her for any length of time. Especially since she kept talking about leaving town.

July 5th, I went down to the unemployment office to reopen my old claim. I got there about 7:15am, when I got to the window, I gave my social security number and was given an application. At the bottom of my application was written $555. I ignored it and sat down to wait.

At 9:15am I was called to the back. I gave my social security number to the lady and she proceeded to tell me my claim had never been closed and that I only had $555 left to receive. I felt faint. I told her that couldn't be, that I had been working for the past five months and showed her my new separation notice. She excused herself to retrieve my paperwork that they kept on file. When she returned, she laid the card on her desk and proceeded to input things into the computer. While I sat there waiting for her to bring up the information she was looking for, I looked at my card. I noticed the card had been signed in my name from May 28 to June 19. I asked the lady if someone there at the unemployment office had signed my card and why? She stated that I had come in and signed for four checks because I didn't receive them. I told her "no hell I didn't", she got up and left to get her supervisor. When the supervisor, Ms. Jones, returned I explained to her that I had been working and had not been receiving unemployment checks, I would have paid off my car (which was repossessed in October). I informed her that I received my last check March 18 and that I had been working since March 11. I then showed her my new separation notice from the law firm. By this time the lady I was seeing had started pulling up the checks to confirm that they had been cashed and dates. I suddenly had this sick feeling in the pit of my stomach. I felt like someone had stolen part of my soul and I was left only as a partial person. I asked them how could someone come in there with just my social security number coming out of their mouth, sign for and receive checks for me or as me. On the 19th of June, Melissa had walked into the unemployment office, as me, with my social security number (it's on the stub that comes with the check) and signed for checks she claimed she had not received. (I had the mail forwarded, the checks are not supposed to be forwarded and had gone back). I was then told that they would have to pull copies of the checks that had been cashed and it would also show where she cashed them.

I would need to verify the signatures and sign affidavits stating that I had not cashed the checks. They made me feel as though I was lying and wasting their time. They took my new address so that I could receive the remainder of the money. I was told that was all they could do at that time. I went home and called Melissa; I didn't want her to know I knew any of this because I wanted her caught. I remembered I had told her I might go down to unemployment, so I called and told her I had gotten a temporary assignment and wouldn't need to go down to unemployment after all. I thought I would be able to call her twice a week, just to keep track of her so that I could tell the authorities where she was so that she could be picked up, when the time came. I found I couldn't do it. I didn't want to hear her voice. I hated her for what she had done to me. I realized that the whole time we shared that house, I was paying the whole amount of the rent, giving her half and she was getting my unemployment checks as well. She had stolen from my children and I wanted no contact with her at all.

THEY THINK I'M LYING

July 8th, I called Ms. Jones, they took a message, she didn't return my call. I was beginning to feel that they felt I was just doing this to get money back that I was not entitle to.

July 9th, I took paperwork to Mrs. Jones, showing her proof that I was at work all day on the day Melissa came in and signed for the checks. I felt I was being ignored. Since I bought this up, I feel as if they think I'm still lying and wondering why I'm taking it this far. I realized at this time that in order for them to listen to me I would have to produce paperwork and do my own police work. I had the office manager from the law firm give me a letter verifying my time of employment with them.

July 10, 11, and 12th, I called Ms. Jones and left messages and got no return calls nor would they put me through to her.

July 13th, I spoke with an investigator at the Dekalb County Office of Investigators. I spoke with a Detective Watts and told him what was going on and asked if there was anything, he could do to move things along. He stated at that time that he couldn't do anything unless I wanted to prosecute. Once I decided to prosecute myself, I would have to take it all the way, there would be no backing out once things got started. The way he said that made me feel like he knew things could get ugly and would be directed at me. I was afraid and decided that I would wait and let the Department of Labor do the prosecuting. He informed me that his hands were tied for now.

My check for July 5th was mailed out to my new address. Well by Wednesday, I noticed I hadn't received any mail since Monday, not even the weekly advertisements. I thought nothing of it and waited for my check. By Friday, my check still hadn't come or any other mail for that matter. Now, what was going on. it was too late to call unemployment because they were already closed.

THANK GOD FOR SPEEDING TICKETS

Saturday, July 14th I woke up about 8:00am, something was bothering me. I laid back down and then it dawned on me, I needed to call the post office. I wanted to catch my postman before he left the post office. I called and asked for the carrier for my apartment complex and gave the name of my apartments. When the carrier answered the phone, I gave him my name and apartment number and he informed me that I had put in a change of address card and that my mail was being forwarded. I just cried; she was still at it. I asked the carrier if he would hold my mail, not forward anymore and I would need a copy of the change of address card signed with my name on it. I briefly explained the situation and he said for me to see him as soon as I got there. At this point I was also mad, but the law works in a disturbing manner. As long as I was patient and let things go through the normal course of action, I was the victim. If I had gone to her and done something to her then she would become the victim and I would be the one in the wrong. I hated it. I went down to the post office and asked to see my carrier and his supervisor. I explained the situation again and was shown the change of address card. It had my mail going from the new address back to the old address I shared with her. The signature was so real. If I didn't know for sure I had not signed it, I would believe that maybe I could have. She had mastered my signature so well that I almost felt I had not a chance in this world to get this matter right. It was very spooky. The card was signed by me and dated June 16, 1991. I never thought I'd hear myself say this but "Thank God for speeding tickets". I remembered the speeding ticket I got on June 16, 1991, while on the way to Florida to be in my friend's wedding. I still had the ticket because I hadn't mailed it in with my payment at the time. When I told them, I wasn't even in town at the time to put in a change, they were willing to give me a copy. The supervisor told me to go and report it to the Stone Mountain Police.

I went to the police department and spoke with the officer in charge. He gave me forms to make a formal statement. After I finished writing out the situation, he informed me that it was out of their jurisdiction and that I would have to go to the Dekalb County Police Department. I was back where I started.

When I got home, I just held my baby and cried. It suddenly dawned on me that if I hadn't discovered all of this and hadn't had the bad vibes about her that I did, I might be "looking" for my baby "today". I really got scared. I even got to the point of being paranoid. I was afraid to leave my apartment. Once I mustered up the guts to leave the apartment to get to my car and was in my car, I was okay. I just had to make myself get out of the door. It took 45 minutes, daily, trying to get up the nerve to open the door and step out. When would it end???

I pulled myself together and called my Godmother, Angie. I asked her if she would take over to the house I shared with Melissa to wait for the mail carrier. I wanted to see if any of my mail was going there today. I didn't want my car to be recognized by anyone. Angie said okay, I took the baby to my sitter and waited to be picked up.

When we got to the street where the house was, we parked down a way from it; to just watch it. I then decided to go and talk with my ex-neighbor, Myrtle. I spoke with Myrtle briefly and she informed me that she had been holding the mail from the old address for Melissa. She also stated that Thursday of that week Melissa came to see her and picked up the mail. She had told Myrtle that I was waiting on a check and it had finally come, so there would be no need for her to continue to hold the mail. Melissa had Myrtle thinking we were sisters and that she was doing this for me.

Angie and I left briefly to go get some lunch to eat while watching for the mail carrier. Upon returning, we ran into him, taking a brief break. I told him the situation and gave him a copy of the police report I had written at the Stone Mountain Police Department. He said he knew something was strange because he was the one forwarding my mail to my apartment. He said then it started coming back and he knew there was no one living in the old address. He said he had been on vacation, that's why the mail had been slow in moving. I had to say "Thank You God" because the regular mail carrier from my apartment, had been on vacation also, that's why the mail from my apartment had not started being forwarded back to the old address until after the Fourth of July. He then handed, me my mail and said he would give the paperwork I had given him to his supervisor to forward it on to the Postal Inspector.

FINALLY, SOMETHING'S HAPPENING

July 17, 1991, Ms. Jones from the unemployment office called; the copies of the cashed checks were in. She stated she needed me to come into the office and verify the signatures and sign an affidavit for each check that had a signature that was not mine.

July 18, 1991, I went down to the unemployment office, I arrived at 7:35am, Ms. Jones was in a meeting, so I had to wait. At 8:15am I was told someone would be with me. While sitting out front waiting, I felt maybe they were starting to take me seriously. I noticed several sudden changes too. At window one, where you received your application to apply for unemployment, they were asking to see your social security card. At window two, where you report address changes, missed checks, etc., they were asking to see the blue card you are given once you are seen and paperwork is collected; but they also wanted to see your social security card and picture ID. I also heard someone tell a person over the phone that they no longer accepted address changes over the phone, you had to come in and show some ID.

At 9:30am, I was finally called to the back. Ms. Jones acted as if at any time I was going to give up the charade and say I changed my mind. I sat down and began looking at the signatures. They were good, they were so good it scared me. I had to keep looking them over two and three times. I almost got to where I wasn't sure, but the dates of the checks kept reminding me that I was working at the time the checks were cashed. I signed a separate affidavit for each copy of a check I did not cash and then I asked if I could have
a copy for myself. It was time I did a little police work of my own. I also had to sign my signature several times so that they could do a handwriting analysis of my handwriting along with the one on the checks. I was told that everything would be sent to the Georgia Bureau of Investigations (GBI). I left there not knowing how long any of this was going to take and tried pulling myself together. Lately I did a lot of crying. I took the copy of the checks and a picture of Melissa to the check cashing place I used to go to. It seems she had been cashing the checks there because I already had a card on file. I talked with a woman who was familiar with seeing me come in and asked her if the lady in the picture had been coming in there to cash checks. She said, "yes". I then asked her if I could see my card on file, every time you cash a check, they write down the date and the amount of the check. I told her the situation and what was going on and she got

the card for me. I looked at the card, Melissa had been cashing my checks on my check cashing card there. It started from the end of March up until she got the last check for $745, that she was able to sign for, as me, at the unemployment office. I also found the missing Public Assistance check; she had cashed that too. The lady I spoke with stated she had noticed that I had stopped buying money orders; I always got money orders when I cashed a check. I asked for a copy of the card and left. Since I was near Angie's house, I went over there to see if Angie's husband, Mac, could look at the two handwritings for me. I felt very empty. I began to wonder if this nightmare was ever going to end. I got to Angie and Mac's home and he was there. I showed him the handwritings, because he worked for the Criminal Investigation Division for the Army. He had to look two or three times just like myself. He finally found somethings he could point out to me to assure me that the signature was definitely forged. I felt a little better, and I also realized that I was not losing my mind. Now all I could do was wait.

July 20th, my temporary agency sent me out on an assignment for 10 days. It helped to take my mind off of my dilemma. Also rent time was coming again I had to do something about getting up some money.

While working at the assignment, I called the Postal Inspector to report the fact that someone at the post office that handled my old address had given a check for $745 to someone posing as me; while my mail was suppose to be forwarded to my new address. The postal inspector stated to me since the

Department of Labor was already investigating the matter; they would let them handle it and just brushed me off.

Since that time, I have noticed that now when you put in a change of address the postal system sends out a confirmation, one to the <u>new</u> address and one to the <u>old</u> address. You have to call and confirm that you have indeed moved. I also called the GBI, the FBI and Secret Service to ask if they kept pictures of women wanted for crimes that were felonies, none of them did.

At the end of July, I went back to Washington, DC to pick up my two older daughters. I was trying to get back on track, but it seemed like my finances were steadily going down hill. When I returned home, the service had another assignment for me that was to last for nine months. I was glad, shouldn't have spent the checks to come until they were actually in my hand (the company I was sent to later laid me off). I wanted to continue to work for the agency in case there was a trial or something. I didn't want to take a job and have to take off in the beginning and risk loosing yet another job.

While waiting for the handwriting analysis to be done, hoping that I would receive all the money stolen from me soon, I just had the hardest time getting jump started. I kept trying to give myself that push to go forward, but I just couldn't get there. This woman had taken on my identity, so to speak. I later found out she had even opened a bank account in my name as well. When I learned of the bank account, I closed my own account. It really made me mad, here I had to close my account in order to cover myself if any checks started bouncing around. Once you are in Chex Systems records, any other banks you may have will be closed as well. I didn't want to be held accountable for two accounts. She was really getting away with a lot.

September 26, 1991, I was told that morning by the Project Manager that this would be my last day. He said there was not as much work as they thought it would be, so they had to let me go. I was working at a construction job site, the company laid me off, not my agency. In fact, they were quite disturbed because they hadn't been informed before I was told. That morning also, I received a call. The amount of money taken was so much that the Georgia Department of Labor had turned the case over to the United States Department of Labor. I was called by Mr. Smith, head of security for the Georgia Department of Labor. He stated that he and a Mr. Walker would like to speak with me. I told them that they could come to the job site where I was working at noon, because the supervisor would be at lunch.

ON TRIAL

Mr. Smith and Investigator Walker arrived at 12:00 noon exactly. We went into a conference room to talk. They introduced themselves and then proceeded to explain why they were there to talk with me. They asked me several questions about Melissa. I gave them the best answers I could, looking them in the eyes. I told them everything I knew about her from living with her. I also told them everything she had ever said to me and things she said that she never thought I'd remember or was even really paying attention to. It's amazing how God will whisper things in your ear at a time when you need it most. I was able to recall conversations with her that to me didn't mean anything, but at this time meant the difference between them believing me or deciding if I had carried this thing far enough and it was time to bring it to an end. They watched me and my expressions, but I never once felt uncomfortable. I had done nothing wrong. I had been wronged and I just wanted it to be made right. I wanted it to be over so that I could start trying to put me back together. They had me look at the signatures again and sign more paperwork. We talked for about an hour. I felt really good when we were done, I felt as though finally, someone believed me and I would see some results, in my favor.

MOVING......................AGAIN

October 1991, I had to move again. I had been out of work since being laid off in September. Not one of the agencies I worked for had anything for me. My car had been repossessed. I couldn't produce my money order receipts to show proof of payments. That's when I realized that must have been how Melissa mastered my signature the way she had. I kept all my money order receipts in my nightstand drawer. I learned I couldn't use my separation papers from the law firm to obtain unemployment, because my old claim was not a year old until November. (The money was gone, but I still had to wait). I moved with my best friend/sister, Barbara and her family.

I met Barbara in 1989 at my doctor's office, she was my nurse. She and I quickly became friends. Our oldest daughters bonded immediately. Her family became my family. I had heard when your birth family turns on you God will send you family from somewhere and this family was the greatest. Through them I learned you don't turn your back on family, no matter what. When they adopted me, I got three brothers and another sister. They all have looked out for my three daughters and myself over the past sixteen years. Being estranged with my birth mother, brother and sisters, I had just decided I would fly solo. Even though by this time I knew my birth father, I couldn't call him and talk with him. I met my oldest brother and youngest brother by my father, we became close, but we lived so far apart we didn't keep in touch that much. My sister and I are so close, our youngest daughters are six months apart and have been raised together.

My adopted family has been so good to me, the love grows stronger and stronger still. We lost our oldest brother in 2003 and we're still feeling it. He too ran a cleaning company. I could call him and ask him anything when it came to helping me with my business. By Bob, I miss you.

Once again, my dear friend and her boys helped me move my furniture. I thanked her for coming to my aid once again. I lived with my sister throughout the rest of October, all of November and the first two weeks of December. I am very grateful to my mom, dad and brothers and sister for taking my and me daughters in like they did. They are my adopted family and had been for over eight years. I thank

God for sending them to me when I met them. No one's ever an outsider with them.

October was just about over, when I received a call from Investigator Walker. He asked me if Melissa had ever mentioned South Dakota. There was a possibility that she might be wanted there too. I told him I couldn't say, I had told him all the places she had mentioned to me. From what Investigator Walker was saying, Melissa had a pattern. She had done this in several other places, meaning cashing other people's checks, and/or getting checks under other people's names and various other fraudulent things. He said whenever she was caught, she always pleaded guilty and paid her fine. Let's hope it goes that way this time. Investigator Walker also informed me that he couldn't tell me anything else at this time because it was not relevant to my case. He did leave me with this, "just be glad you never left your kids alone with her". Boy did that scare me, she always baby-sat for me. My girls were alone with her often. I had all kinds of horrible things running through my mind. I had to Thank God over and over for keeping them safe and keeping angels around them when they were alone with her. The call made me feel good and bad; I was just glad they finally had something to go on and I wasn't being looked at as if I were the culprit. When my daughters got home from school, I hugged them both, feeling grateful that nothing had happened to them because of me and some wrong decision making.

WHAT A THANKSGIVING

November 1991, around the second week, I received a call from Investigator Walker. He told me he was impressed with me when we spoke in September and that he believed me. He also stated that he had given the Georgia Department of Labor the okay to reissue me the money from the stolen checks. All I could say once again was "Thank You God".

Thanksgiving was nice. I had a lot to be thankful for. I was surrounded by friends, *true* friends and family. I had looked at a house the week before and had explained the situation to the Realtor. She said if I was to get my money back, call her. I called her and told her to give me two weeks for the check to get to me.

On December 2nd I had the keys in my hand. On December 14th, my daughters and I moved into our own home. The week before Christmas, a Detective Watts called me; he stated that Melissa had pleaded not guilty. My first thoughts, she had broken the pattern. Then I remembered Investigator Walker had mentioned her possibly being wanted in South Dakota; maybe she was buying time. He told me I would be subpoenaed to a hearing sometime in January or February. I asked why? He stated he didn't know, but that the hearing would be informal and not to worry. Easy for him to say, I thought.

FACING HER

January 1992, I was subpoenaed to appear at a hearing for Melissa. I was uncomfortable, I hadn't seen her since June 1991. I still had bad feelings about her. I didn't want any kind of confrontation with her or her sisters, who were known for fighting. The hearing was for the following week.

Melissa was being charged with *"Forgery in the First Degree"*. She had other charges against her too, but they didn't pertain to me. I arrived early and sat down to wait. Melissa arrived with her boyfriend and another girl. I had seen this girl before; Melissa was the only friend she had. I had been told that Melissa had witnesses, I guess they were it. The woman who had identified Melissa from a picture for me had also been subpoenaed, she was to be a witness for the state. They had us sit in this little room so that we couldn't hear each other's testimony.

After what seemed like an eternity, I was called to testify. Melissa had an attorney; he tried very hard to make it look as though I had been lying about the whole matter. Her lawyer asked me how I was collecting unemployment and Public Assistance. He tried to make it look like I was intentionally defrauding the government. I explained to the judge that when I informed the intake worker that I intended to apply for unemployment, she stated with emphasis that I only had to report "earned" income. I had already worked for, the unemployment, that was why I had not reported it. I also knew their computers were tapped into the Department of Labor's computers and they could easily find out. No matter what or how he asked me a question I did not stutter or loose my composer. I think I made him angry to the point of frustration. He wanted me to give him my current address in court. I informed the judge that I didn't trust Melissa and that I would not give my address out loud because I feared for my daughters' safety. He told her attorney that I could leave it with the court, only if he needed it for business reasons. He couldn't say why he wanted it, he just wanted it. I told the judge everything I had told Investigator Walker and Mr. Smith; I was then told I could leave. I was not asked for my address again. The other witness for the state, the woman who had identified Melissa for me didn't testify. At the last minute she decided she wasn't sure if Melissa was the woman, she had cashed the checks for or not. I guess she was threatened once I left the little room we had been in or their appearance was enough to scare her. So, with that testimony out of the window and Melissa's two witnesses not holding up, I was told nothing could be done until her handwriting analysis came back. For the time being I was done, I asked Detective Watts if he would walk me to my car because I was afraid to walk to it alone.

While we walked to my car, he stated he remembered me coming in to see him earlier, when it all started. He remembers I wanted someone to lean on the Department of Labor to hurry and get the copies of the canceled checks. It's ironic because even though I decided I didn't want to proceed alone and left his office lost, confused and frightened that day; he still ended up handling the case. Then he stated that when he got the case file <u>her</u> name looked familiar. So, he pulled her up in the computer. He said when he received the warrant to arrest her it all came back to him. Four years prior to this time, he was the arresting officer that picked her for credit card fraud, a felony. The police had been called to her house for beating up one of her children. My question to him was "why was she not in jail?", had she been in jail, our paths would never have crossed. All he could say was "I don't know".

February 1992, I have written President Bush in reference to getting the back-child support due me by my first ex-husband (he was $20,000 in the rear). I marked the envelope "Help from a registered voter" and sent it registered mail. I had decided I would not try to go back to work until the summer because I let my daughters continue to go to school out by the old address. I dropped them off and picked them up daily. I had come to see that they needed me at that time with all the changes they had been through. My oldest was about to graduate from seventh grade and my fifth grader had started having serious growing pains.

LIFE GOES ON

March 1992, I called Detective Watts to see how the case was going. He informed me that 95% of the handwritings were proved to be Melissa's, I forgot I had cashed the check sent to me when my mail was being forwarded when I moved away from her in June 1991.

Now we had to wait for her to be arraigned. **ME,** I'm doing better. Finally, but slowly, getting all of me back into to place. Getting on my feet slowly. Today I received my first child support check from the courts in Washington, DC. They now have a garnishment in place for my ex-husband. This means a lot, now I can stay home until summer and feel comfortable about doing so. God is truly good. I've just learned that my seventh grader will be graduating as valedictorian, so-to-speak, at her school; it has truly made a difference my being able to be there. Maybe I can start my own business and not have to work for anyone else again, we'll see. Yes, I am leery of meeting new people, but I guess that feeling will pass, one day.

July 1992, I called Detective Watts to see what was going on so that I could close this book and really put my mind at ease. I was informed that Melissa would be appearing before a judge around the first or second week of August. I told him I would give him a call at the end of August or the first of September to see what the judge would rule.

September 1992, I called Detective Watts and was informed that Melissa was given three years probation, a $2,500 Order of Restitution (to pay back the Department of Labor), and a $1,000 fine. Well it was finally over. I could really go on. I felt like part of me had been restored. I'm whole once again. It was rough, I've had to develop a new signature block, this one I'm sure no one will be able to copy. I'm starting fresh and I feel good, "Thank You Lord".

JUST FOR THE RECORD

I would like to add this. I became one of the homeless after losing my job, going through what you just read about, and losing a second job as well as my home. I say that to say this: a lot of our homeless are not homeless because they want to be or because they're lazy. With all the knocks society throws at you it makes you <u>want</u> to give up. **NO**, some of the homeless are not homeless because they don't give a <u>Damn</u> or <u>Don't</u> want to pay their rent, etc. When it gets to the point where you can hardly pay or even afford the necessities...........rent, food, lights, water, gas, it gets to be a bit much, especially with a family looking to you for these things. You start to ask yourself - why should I keep trying. Sometimes that "next" GUT PUNCH from life makes some people feel like they may as well stay down so that they don't have to <u>keep</u> getting knocked down. The system shuffles you around, full of excuses why they can't help you. You don't want your family to know how bad it is for you; some people know that their family wouldn't care anyway. Soon you just say, "to hell with it all". The only reason <u>I</u> didn't give up is because I realized our children often follow in our footsteps. I knew that if I quit, my daughters would or might end up quitters too, I didn't want that. Plus, I held fast to my faith in God. He hasn't let me down yet. I also learned to ask Him to speak to me <u>loud</u> with my answers so that I don't miss what it is I'm supposed to hear or take it wrong because I missed a word. I have just taken a permanent job, it's nice to have benefits. I always believe God puts me in places and positions to learn things that will help me run my own business someday. This company is small, 15 people, and I'm learning that if you're good at the services you offer, you can be successful -- no matter how "small" you are. Things are looking better day to day. I've bought another car, was able to pay for its cash, no note - Yeah! My two oldest daughters still to this day have not a clue as to how bad a person they had been living with and that they could have been in danger daily. They're happy, one wants to be an engineer and the other a doctor; truly growing into fine young ladies and cheering me on constantly. The baby is walking and trying to talk. She's happy with me.

Proverbs 18:24
        A man that has friends must show himself friendly and there is a friend that
        sticketh closer than a brother.
                THANKS: Denise, Doreen, Jeanette, Demetria,
        my daughters, Kita, Keisha and Joc

I would also like to say this:

To Society ---------- I was once told you can't judge a man unless you've walked a mile in his moccasins. ----- You need to put this up somewhere visible where you can see it when you start to judge the homeless or people down on their luck. I'm sure you've been down on your luck before, did any one judge you?
To The Homeless ---------- Find the Lord, put Him in your life. Hold fast to your faith in Him and keep

HOPE alive in your heart. He <u>won't</u> let you down.
GOD BLESS YOU ALL.

It was 1987, I was living in Birmingham Alabama after a car accident in Georgia. I was thrown into entrepreneurship when my 1st ex-husband was stationed overseas in Germany. He stopped my child support, even though it was court ordered. When I got to Birmingham, I knew one person, I was afraid to drive, so I made sure I was near a bus stop, but this place felt like I had gone back in time. I learned a lot living there for the 2 years I was there. I applied for food stamps and Medicaid so the girls and I could receive medical help if needed, until I obtained employment. The Medicaid came in handy, as I had to have my 3rd breast lump removed, I had one in 1977 – a junior in high school and I had the 2nd one 2 yrs. later after my first daughter was born. Surgery went well, I did not let them put me to sleep, when I told the anesthesiologist that I did not was to be put out. Why did he say to me that's good, Americans always want to be put out for surgery, they don't all require it and you don't know what kind of day I'm having…………..really?

As I looked for work, with a new resume, it was hard. After months of applying, I realized, I was in a place where my resume meant nothing. I was in a place where my character and my family were what they wanted to know; I had no family there.

After a while, I got this wild idea to work for myself………………………………………………………
…………whaaaaaaaaaaaaaaaaaaaaat?
I had bought my computer with me, back then it was a 256 desktop that used 5 x 7 floppy disk; and a printer that printed in pixels, YES OLD, I truly have watched computers evolve FOR REAL!!!!

I started two businesses, the first business, WAKE UP WITH YOU? was a wake-up service. I advertised in the newspaper and picked up three customers. They paid me to wake them up for work, 3 different times, 3pm, 11pm and 3am, Mmm Hmm.

The second business was contracting myself out to one-man businesses. AT & T had just started the second line on one phone, so I used it to forward their phones to me; it had a different ring. The shoe repair and the dry cleaners, whenever they had to lock their door to leave the store, I answered their phones. I also charged them to do letters, contracts and light bookkeeping. Then I expanded the business and took it to the printer. At the time, magazines, newspapers and other big print materials, were printed by way of having the lettering laid out and then inked by a roller and then run so that the letters, story, ad, etc. was printed on a roll of paper and cut for whatever it was for; a newspaper, magazine, etc.
Soooooooooooooooooooooo when they had customers who wanted their print job "rushed" they contacted me, and I printed it from my printer at home. How about that??????? Working from home before working from home was a THING! I've also watched printer EVOLVE ALSO, no I'm not OLD, I'm SEASONED!!!!! The first time I ever said I wanted to work for myself was in 1981, I surprised myself as I didn't know where that came from. As I looked back on the Covington family, my maternal grandfather's side of the family, I remember, we quite a few entrepreneurs; my great aunt Florestine Dickerson, my cousin Lenny, my uncle Pearson.

Going back to D.C. in 1983 and going back to work for the government and trying private industry, working on capital hill, was made me decide to try this business ownership thing for real. So, in 1986, Mother's Day, I packed myself up and moved to Atlanta, GA, for some reason, I felt being Black I would have a better chance there to open a business.

Back to Birmingham, AL; working for myself was exhilarating and it allowed me to call my time, so I was there for my daughters. I did finally obtain employment at the University of Alabama (UAB) and the plan was to work for a year and go back to Georgia. Well, I ended up working 2 years and returned to Atlanta, GA with a second husband in 1989. We didn't last long, 18 months and he had to go, he was used to being a big fish in a little pond in Birmingham, and he couldn't swim with the bigger fish in the larger entity of water. But God, I didn't start another business right away, but in 1994 God finally said OK and gave me a business to open; thus, the birth of NO ORDINARY KLEANING.

A NEW DAY HAS DAWNED

Early 1994, I filed my divorce papers myself by publication (putting it in the paper for 30 days), it was granted in July 1994. I was allowed to go back to my maiden name.

In April of 1994 I was laid off with my oldest daughter starting to look at colleges. I still wanted to own my own business, so I went to God. I told Him I needed and wanted Him to tell me what to do. My unemployment had been denied so I had an appeal in; no child support from either ex-husband, what was I to do? I told God I knew He would have an answer for me by the end of the week. If it wasn't for me to own a business than point me to the ideal job that would allow me to take care of my family with no hardship.

Well it's Saturday morning, since that conversation and Kita and I are about to go and look at a college. She falls to sleep, and I start talking to God. Okay Lord, it's Saturday, nothing's happened and I haven't heard from you yet. What am I going to do? Bills are due, I see no money in sight. We get to the college, tour and have lunch. The next half is splitting up to go to separate panels to get our questions answered. When I sat down, the room disappeared, and it was me and this voice. It said I was to open another construction final cleaning company. I said, "Are you sure?" I was told to name the company N.O.Ch.(NOK), for "No Ordinary Chleaning", (it was changed to NO ORDINARY KLEANING, when I moved the family and the business to Jacksonville, FL. I was told to hire the homeless, provide transportation and a meal while they worked. I asked "why?" I was reminded of my bout with homelessness. I had no car at the time and public transportation didn't go out to the areas where the better jobs were. Feed them because if they were not with me, they would be in someone's lunch line at a shelter, etc. I said, "okay, I would do this", I was so excited. When the room came back the panel was over, I had missed it. I looked down and had written notes of all that was told to me. Kita and I headed home; my mind was racing. I was excited about starting up this new business; as this was the same as the business, I dissolved in 1992. I got home and checked my mail. There was a letter from the unemployment office, my appeal had been approved. All money would be retroactive. I would now have the money to get the paperwork done to legalize N.O.Ch.

I got the paperwork done for the business; I was ready to go. Even though I was in church and I read my bible, I didn't know God and His word. I didn't know I should have waited on God to make provision to run N.O.Ch.; I didn't know He would do that. It is a year later; my baby girl is now in kindergarten. I am working on an indefinite temporary assignment.

I just got my first contract with BEERS Construction Company. I have been awarded a contract at the place where my temporary assignment is located. God is good and I'm excited. I needed workers, so I went to the unemployment office. In Georgia at this time, if someone was offered a job and they refused the job; their unemployment check was stopped. I developed a working relationship with the person in charge of the homeless veterans.

We did a great job and I was given my trademark "pastel pink" hardhat. I got a few more jobs after that then things just halted.

Late 1994, I started a long-distance relationship with someone who had been my best friend for about 18 years. Sometimes it works better to just keep the friendship just that. Some male friends aren't meant to be relationships; it didn't work out. I wish him the best and   thanks for all the positive words over the years that always made me feel worthy.

It's 1996, I've had several ups and downs; but have kept God in front of me always, while getting closer to Him daily. Earlier I started a business, with a partner, and had to dissolve it in 1992. God is the best partner you can have unless He sends you someone who you will work well with and who has goals in mind similar to yours. Always and still wanting to be an entrepreneur; God hadn't yet told me, "No way, keep your day job", yet. Now when I want an answer from Him on anything, before I proceed, I go on a three day fast. I don't eat or drink anything during that time. Depending on the weather by the second day I may have to drink some water; but without fail, by the end of it I've got an answer.

I'M A NEW MOTHER...................... AGAIN!

Their names are Keith and Aaron, my sons. Keith is eight and Aaron is three. I've decided to adopt them so that Joc, now 5, going on 6, would have some company to share things with. Kita is now 17 and Keisha is almost 14. They are busy with high school and the things that go with that. Sometimes too busy for their little sister, she started feeling like an only child. I also was not ready for the other two girls to leave home and give me the "empty nest" syndrome.

HOW IT ALL BEGAN

Joc came to me in September of 1995; whining about wanting a baby brother. Everyone in her Pre-K class at school had a baby brother, except for Alexandria, she had a baby sister. Every week she came to me with the same thing. I told her I couldn't give her a baby brother. I told her I had thought about adopting but later on down the road, not right now. She asked what adoption was, so we talked about it and she said she would think about it. She decided that wouldn't work, the baby had to come out of my stomach. I knew that would be impossible, especially being single.

One day she came to me and said, "I know what my brothers name is going to be". I said, "what?" She said "Jonathan Christopher". I said, "Joc I told you I can't have any more babies". She got real upset. Then Keisha said to her, "even if mommy could have a baby, Joc, it could be another girl". Joc said, "Oh no, I have all the sisters I can handle. What about this adoption thing mommy?" Keisha said, "It's like shopping but for a child, you get to choose what <u>you</u> want". Joc said, "okay mommy let's do that". She said she wanted a baby brother two years younger than her and dark as her. She requested dark because the two big girls and I are fair skinned. I told her I would see what I could find out and get back with her. I guess you might be wondering why I talk to this little girl as if she were another adult. I have always spoken to and treated my children as though their feelings and opinions counted; sometimes they have sometimes they haven't. We have the kind of relationship that has made it easy for them to come to me and talk about anything; something I never had with my birth mother. Children have plenty of sense and if exercised right they will be good for you and to you in years to come.

I was totally lost as to where to start looking first or who to call. I didn't want to do foster parenting, because those children are only placed for a brief time, every now and then it might go into years but that's not guaranteed. I'd had always had adoption on my mind but I was not in the market to "buy" a child nor did I want to feel as if I had. I knew I couldn't afford a lot of money for attorneys, etc. I had heard the adoption process takes so long and could be expensive. I stood in the kitchen just wondering; I dropped it from my list of things to think about and started washing my breakfast dishes. Once again, I am unemployed, but happy about it, because Joc was in Pre-K and I got to walk her to school and pick her up and meet other at home moms, every day. I was home and dinner was ready when Kita and Keisha got in, it was nice. I learned that your children need you more as they get older, and I wanted to be there for all three of mine as much and as often as I could.

ROOTS

One day, after walking Joc to school, I had the radio on and was taken out of my daze by the interview going on at the time on the radio. An adoption agency was on V103, a radio station in Atlanta, that had always given me valuable information in the past. I stopped and listened; her name is Toni. It seems she had opened her own adoption agency, specializing in African American adoptions of children from the ages two and up. She wanted to educate African Americans on how easy adopting could be, but also to try and get as many African American children out of foster care as she could. The thing that has always stuck with me was what she said at the end of the interview, which was, "we don't care if you live at home with your own momma, we just want people who want to be good parents". I thought I could do that; I took the number for "ROOTS" and called right away. They said they would send me some information and that an orientation was coming up in the next week. I was interested and somewhat excited.

I received the information the same week and called to register for the orientation. I went on a Saturday and met the lady from the radio. She had such a spirit that it made you want to take all the children she had to offer. At the orientation I learned the classes would be ten weeks long, one night a week or on Saturday. They told us everything that would go on in the classes, I was ready to commit. I went home and talked with my daughters about it and we all agreed it was something we wanted to do. We had Christmas and closed out 1995 in church New Year's Eve.

MY TURN NOW

My M.A.P.P. (**M**odel **A**pproach to **P**artnership and **P**arenting) classes started the second week of January 1996. These classes are geared towards getting you in touch with your self. They also educated you about the potential problems the child or children may have that would be coming into your home. After going to my first class, I went home and told my daughters how it went and told them about this catalog. It's kept at the libraries and it contains pictures of children available for adoption; it's called "My Turn Now". We decided we would go to the library on the next day and take a look.

MY SONS, THEIR BROTHERS

The next evening, the girls and I went to the library to look at the catalog. We decided we would pick three little boys, turning three that year. We would get the one left when I finished the classes. We looked and looked, and it didn't look like we had a lot to choose from. Suddenly, Kita and Keisha said, "mommy, they're the ones, these are our brothers". I said, "there's two of them". Kita said, "we're almost at the end of the book. All the children are either featured with a sibling or are older than what we are looking for". I looked at the boys and read the caption under their picture. It seemed they were living in separate fosters homes, and it was a must that they be adopted together. It did state that a single parent was acceptable. I looked at my daughters, they were excited, especially Joc. I said, "Well, they'll be coming in on your territory, if you can handle it so can I". We xeroxed the page and took our two new family members to-be home.

ARE THEY FREE?

The next day I called ROOTS and asked if they would check on "my sons'" availability. When this is done, they check to see if the birth parents' rights had been relinquished, etc. Sometimes even though children are in the catalog someone else has inquired and they're put on hold for that person or people. In doing this there is no confusion with more than one family waiting on the same child/children. I'm sure my way of describing the process may sound a little disturbing but I'm trying to say it as simple as I can to get my points across. I got my call back and was told they were still available; the girls and I are really excited now; classes can't be over soon enough. We put their picture on the refrigerator so that we could look at them every day. We said "good morning and good night" to them daily. I kept plenty of prayer over them, constantly asking my Father in Heaven to keep them safe until they came home.

Classes are interesting, so were the people I took class with. There was one other single woman like myself, one single man, the rest were couples. The classes put you in touch with your feelings, your strengths and what needs you should build up. During the classes I learned that a lot of things I had applied during my on-the-job parenting with my 14-year-old over the years, were being taught to us in class. I thanked God for the lessons before hand. We were taught 15 behavior methods to use other than spanking. We were told stories of things our adopted child or children might put us through and how to handle it. I also made some very good friendships that I felt would be lasting. In class they would often emphasis how important it was to have a support system once your adopted child or children came home. One night after returning home from class, my daughters cornered me and asked me what the boys' last name would be when they came home. I said they would automatically be given my last name "Covington". My daughters decided that night that they wanted their last names changed to Covington so that our household would have only one name. The big girls had my first ex-husband's last name and my baby girl had my second ex-husband's last name. So, I started working on a name change for them.

Joc was so excited, she quickly learned to spell Covington. She went to school the next day and started putting it on her papers. The teacher stopped her and asked her why she was writing that name. She said it was going to be the name of her brothers. The teacher informed her she could not put this name on her papers until she saw paperwork saying it was legal. Joc came home from school livid. I asked what was wrong and she told me what happened at school. The next day I went to class with her and told the teacher what was going on. I asked her if Joc could write Covington on her papers, and she said not until it was legal. Now I was mad. I said okay and took Joc to the side and told her she couldn't write Covington for now. So, for the rest of the school year Joc refused to write her last name on her papers. She wrote her name on all her papers "Joc O." with no last name. It was too funny. Don't tell me children don't have a "mind" of their own. The girls started the new school year as Covingtons. My oldest would graduate from high school using both her last names with a hyphen. I let my daughters attend one class with me so that they could get any questions they might have answered first-hand.

The night I took Joc to the class with me, she already had her question ready. She wanted to know if we could give the child a new name. After we had been in class about 40 minutes, Joc raised her hand. She was not noticed. She kept her hand raised, then took her other hand and held up her elbow to keep her hand raised. Finally, she looked up at me and asked, "Do they do you like this too?" I did my best not to laugh. Finally, her hand was acknowledged, and she was told we could give him a new middle name. She was excited.

Soon classes were over. I had filled out all the necessary paperwork as I felt sure this was what I wanted to do. I had my fingerprint check done and took my physical before Easter rolled around. We were ready now all we had to do was wait.

WHAT'S TAKING SO LONG

And wait we did. Mother's Day came and went, and June was fast approaching. We had two graduations to attend out of town. I wanted to take the opportunity to introduce my sons to family up north. My adopted family in Georgia were excited and my sister that I'm closest to, had three girls like me with our youngest daughters being six months apart.

June is here, school is closing, and we have heard nothing from the county that the boys are living in. What's wrong???? Daily Joc is saying, "mommy, when are my brothers coming home?" I couldn't answer her. I called the agency every week and they were waiting to hear too. One day the person working with me stated that the county my boys were in had not released any children for adoption to date. They moved so slow that people always changed their minds and picked other children. I was told I might want to think about that and look at some other children. I said I would not, those boys were mine I didn't want to choose any more. I told her that our vacation, etc. was being held up because we wanted to take the boys with us. What could I do? I was given the direct number to the social worker of my sons. I called him and he informed me that I had been approved to have the boys. I said okay and waited some more.

I NEED SOME HELP

It's the 4th of July, we've missed the graduations and any out-of-town trip. My family is starting to wonder if I was still going to get them. I spoke with my son's social worker again and asked if they had changed their minds about letting me have Keith and Aaron. He said no I was still going to get them it's just taking some time. I later learned that he was not familiar with the adoption process so that was part of the hold up.

It came to me to write a letter. I called ROOTS and informed them what I wanted to do; I also asked them if they minded if I mentioned the agency in my letter. I was told that that would be okay but to let them see the letter first before I sent it off; they even gave me the name of the person the letter should be addressed to.

I penned my letter July 10. It went something like this (excerpts):
HELP!!!!

My name is Cherron and I am writing to see if you can help me. I am in the process of adopting
two little boys. They are presently in foster care in this county and I've run into a snag. I thought this whole thing was
about helping the children, especially African American children, definitely the boys.
I read in the newspaper that Department of Family and Children Services (DFCS) had launched a campaign to get at least
400 children out of the system before the year was out. Have the 400 been selected and can I look at that list if

it's going to be impossible for me to get my sons from this county. The article talked about the difficulty in finding
        African American families to place these children with and how we as African Americans don't look out for our own.
        I am African American - I want to adopt <u>two boys</u> out of the system; can you help me.

I faxed the letter to the agency to look it over; I was also copying two people in Congress for my district and to the state representative for my district. Someone was going to help me, I was sure. Toni called me from the agency and made two corrections and told me to send it on. I faxed it to everyone that it was to go to. In an hour the person I sent the letter to called me at work (yes, I'm back in the working force once again). She apologized for the trouble and said she would get to the bottom of the problem and call me back; someone would be calling me soon.

July 18th I was finally on my way to my staffing. This is a meeting with the social worker of the child/children, his supervisor, the person in charge of adoptions in the DFCS office and the foster parents. Here is where the question and answer session goes on between everyone.

My daughters, my agency worker from ROOTS and myself drove two and a half hours to get to the staffing and to hopefully see my sons in person. My sons were biological brothers but had never lived together, that was why it was stressed that they be adopted together. Keith was 7 going on 8 and had been in two foster homes, the last one for three years. Aaron had just turned 3 and had been in five foster homes with some abuse; not that there was anything wrong with him. He just got some bad breaks with adults who had issues within they had not resolved within themselves. After all the questions had been asked, we were given the opportunity to do a blind visit (we could see them thru a one-way glass window, but they couldn't see us).

They were adorable. Keith was dark as Joc had requested, Aaron was the complexion of myself and the two big girls. We watched them for about 20 minutes and then had to go back to the meeting. I was then asked when did I want to start my visits with my sons. You have to do three visits before they actually move in with you. I gave them dates for the next three weeks, school was going to be opening soon and I didn't want Keith to have too big of an adjustment to make all at one time.

WE FINALLY GET TO MEET THEM

Our first visit was July 27 - just for the day. We got into town and the social worker met us. We went to meet Aaron first. He had been taken from a couple he was with and had just recently been placed in this foster home. He was so adorable; the girls and I wanted to take him home right then. He was cautious at first until I took out my camera and took a picture of him; that's when he decided he wanted to sit on my lap. I picked him up and knew right away he was mine. He was still in diapers but was being potty trained. The foster mother couldn't tell me much, he had only been with her for three months. His favorite foods were french fries, potato salad, and peanut butter sandwiches. I was told he had a sensitive stomach and couldn't eat some things. After about an hour there we asked if Aaron could go with us over to the foster home Keith was in. I had packed food in the hopes of having a picnic with my sons. While still at Aaron's foster home, I gained a new respect for the social worker. He was working that Sunday; he had placed a little boy two weeks before, in the same home Aaron was staying in. He was bringing his belongings over that day.

Keith is quiet and didn't warm up to us until it was almost time to leave. He is small for his age, they both were, and he likes Sega Genesis. He warmed up to Joc immediately, he wanted to show her around and took her outside; it was just what she wanted. She was being blessed with a brother two years younger than her as she requested, but also a big brother two years older than she was. We ended up bringing our food into the house and putting it with the dinner Keith's foster mom had cooked. It was nice, I liked the way they had raised Keith, he was mannerable, he had a bedtime schedule that coincided with the one Joc had, it all seemed really good. We talked about his favorite foods, and the fact that he liked to read. We took pictures with everyone in it and then it was time to go; my heart hurt to have to leave them. But it wouldn't be too much longer.

LEAVING WITHOUT THEM

On the way home I asked the girls what did they think. They all couldn't wait for them to come home. None of us had any misgivings about bringing these two little boys into our lives and our home. Keisha told me Keith had talked with her and asked her some questions. Being as old as he was, he knew the difference between foster care and being adopted and it seemed he couldn't wait to come home.

August 3rd and 4th we went back for our overnight visit; the boys got to stay with us in a hotel. We had pizza for lunch, mutual agreement with the three little ones and went shopping. It was nice, we had dinner in the hotel. Sunday, we had breakfast and rode around town for a while. I had agreed to help the foster mother give Keith his 8th birthday party, which was also a farewell to him by people who had been in his life for the past three years. We all had fun; everyone was warm towards my family. They all had good feelings about Keith coming to live with us.

August 9-11th my sons came to their new home to-be for a weekend with us. They had their own room, new beds and dressers. Most children in foster care hardly ever own too many things that they are the first to have; Keith was excited. That weekend Aaron learned to climb the stairs alone. They met the kids in the neighborhood and played outside. Joc had already briefed the children and told them her brothers were coming home and not to say they were adopted, because they were her brothers for keeps. We stayed home all weekend so that the boys could become familiar with the surroundings. They left Sunday evening with four days of waiting before they would be home for good.

ON THE WAY HOME

August 15th, 1996, was the day. Joc and I were on our way to pick up her brothers and my sons. We arrived at the DFCS office around 4:00 with a worker from ROOTS. It took an hour to do paperwork, and Joc did get to give Aaron the middle name Christopher. We didn't like his middle name, and these would be the names on the new birth certificates I would receive later, with my name on them, once we were final. I left Keith's name the same since he was so much older and already knew it well. Soon we were able to go and pick up the boys. We got Keith first, bought his bike and a big wheel he wanted Aaron to have, and all his little belongings. He hugged his foster mom and dad and the dog. I informed the foster parents that they were more than welcome to stay in touch with Keith and they said okay. Next, we picked up Aaron, he didn't have much to bring. I had been blessed enough to be given bags of clothes by a lady I worked with for Aaron and in my excitement, I had been buying clothes for the both of them for about two months.

AND NOW....................................

It's been months, we haven't had any horrible moments, I've been blessed. Keith went through an adjusting period getting used to having Aaron around I don't know when he was told he had a little brother. The only time he saw Aaron was when the social worker picked them up once a month to spend the day with them. Keith had always been the youngest and only boy in his foster homes. He got along with Joc as though he had always been with us. Aaron adjusted well. He had never had any mommy bonding so just sitting and holding him warmed him up to me right away. He had his moments when he would scream because he couldn't have his way, so I would scream with him. He finally stopped; he decided it wasn't working. For Christmas we were featured in the newspaper for the adoption and for the fact that this was the boys first Christmas together. I've learned raising boys is very different from raising girls. Boys need more of you, reassurance, attention and more love.

HOMELESS ....AGAIN

In 1996, before the boys came home, I was in the process of buying a house. I went in on a rent to own deal, with 18 months to get myself credit worthy. I was in the house five months and called to tell the company I was ready to buy the house I was in. While I was at home, enjoying my boys and letting them get somewhat adjusted, the company called me at work and left a voice message. They cancelled my contract without any explanation why. I called them, and got the run around, I waited for paperwork in the mail explaining why my contract was cancelled and nothing came. In September I moved out, since I didn't know what was happening. The $800 a month I was paying was supposed to go toward my closing, since I would not be closing, I didn't want to stay. Had a very uneasy feeling something was not right. We moved in with a friend of mine in her two-bedroom apartment. I was in need of a car and now a place to live. I went to God, I asked Him why was this happening again. The only difference between this time and the time in 1990 was I was able to work and did have a job. I applied for several houses and some apartments, I kept being turned down, for different reasons; too many children, they didn't rent to single person families, etc. After two weeks with my friend, I was able to buy a van and two weeks after that I secured a townhouse apartment. Things were looking up. Sometimes we go through things so that others faith can be strengthened, in this case my two oldest daughters. The boys are still adjusting but doing well. After I got settled into our new home, I pulled out the papers from the house I had left. I started remembering things like the water being cut off twice, because the previous renter left owing a bill. When I went down to the water company with my paperwork, they told me I had been the fourth person in that house in a 6-month period of time. Another time, I had a leak under the carpet. I called a plumber to come out and was told the house should not have passed inspection. An ordinary garden hose had been hooked up to the air conditioning unit and the condensation pan was overflowing. The plumber told me if it had been a leak in a pipe, they might have had to jack hammer the cement foundation up to get to the pipes; he ended it by saying "my homeowners' insurance would have paid for it". That's what made me move, I wasn't the homeowner. The next day I went down to the State Office and looked up the company. They were incorporated, but had changed their name five times, but never their articles. On top of that, they were not suppose to be taking monies and claiming to be selling houses, they were only supposed to be educating people on how to fix their credit so that they would be able to get a mortgage to buy a house. I went to the investigative reporters at the news, I went to Better Business Bureau and others, no one would listen. So, I sued them for my down payment and won by default. I filed paperwork that would enable me to garnish their bank account. It took two years and just as I was able to serve my paperwork to their bank, the business was put in the news. I was out of town and my daughters called me and told me the business had been found out and had been broken up. All bank accounts, etc. were frozen, so my garnishment was no good. When I returned to town, I had gotten some paperwork from a lawyer; stating that I was a creditor named in the bankruptcy the company had filed. I filled out my paperwork and sent it back. That was five years ago, to date have not received any monies, I am what is called an unsecured debt; we are the last to be paid if there is anything left.

WE'RE FINALLY LEGAL

The adoption was finalized in October of 1998, and we moved to Florida. I've taken a job but just for a little while. I got the business underway in September of 1999. I realized my three little ones needed me at home. There's too much lurking out there for me not to give them my undivided attention; at their schools and at home. Working for myself enables me to start and stop working as I choose. I decided a long time ago if I didn't accomplish anything else in this lifetime, I was going to be a good parent, not perfect, but the best I could be. Being a mommy and not just somebody's mother has meant a lot to me. I know now, when the business does take off, it is to be my ministry; helping other homeless people, who are ready to pick themselves back up and make another go at it. I will also be bringing folks to the Lord, as He is the only someone who can help you pick yourself up. In reading spiritual materials and books I read "Success is not measured by wealth but by what you give back". This is what made me decide to be obedient and hire the homeless, since I had been there myself. Am I finished with children? only God knows. I know I have one college graduate and one in the Air Force who will finish her degree while in there.

The three little ones, who give me joy and heartache, life is good, because I will do well with the help of my Heavenly Father. As long as I listen to Him and let Him order my steps and move on His say-so I will prosper in every way.

BYE!

The last part of this book is dedicated to:
      the people at ROOTS
      My new family of adoptive parents that I took my classes with.

Thanks for making me feel like I belong.

A NEW BEGINNING

It is the summer of 1998; I'm moving to Florida. I asked God and He said as long as I was moving there for the right reasons, yes, I could go. Then He showed me this lady's face in the glass on the bus.

I knew whoever she was I was supposed to help her in some way, once I got to Florida. I'm living in Jacksonville, Florida, I like it here......so far.
I decided not to date any more after a failed relationship. I noticed I had to be careful about dating, because my sons are watching. They will pick up on any negative ways I let a man handle me and they would try it themselves. Boys put their moms up so high that if you fall it's a hard road to get back to where you were with them before. So, staying out of the dating game at that time worked for me.

I like Florida, I'm not sure whether or not I will start the business here, but I do know that I want to do something other than work for someone else. I've checked the paper and there are a lot of cleaning companies starting up every day, but that doesn't mean it won't work for me. We'll see.

The summer isn't that hot but there are fires sprouting everywhere, ash is falling like snow; it's sort of scary. My three little ones are with me, Keisha stayed in Georgia to graduate with her class and Kita is in her second year of college. They will be here for Thanksgiving and Christmas.

THE LADY IN THE GLASS

I met the lady whose face I saw in the glass today. She is Mrs. "B". I was walking past the front of her house, and she called to me. She is so nice; we introduced ourselves and started talking about business. I found out she owned a childcare center and worked full time for the school board. I got to where I looked forward to seeing her and talking with her daily. School was about to start, and she asked if I had picked a school for my three little ones. I told her I didn't have a clue as to where to send them. She suggested the school she worked at. She ran the cafeteria there and also at four other schools. She said I could tell the school we were family and to see if they could attend the school since she would be there. Mrs. "B" offered to take my kids in with her in the morning and asked me to help out at her center for a while until I found a job. She wanted to make some changes and asked me to help. I became her consultant, handling human resources, public relations, marketing, and more. Whatever she needed I found out about it and took care of it for her. Mrs. "B" and I got so close she became another "momma" for me. She was good to me and my children. I decided there was nothing I wouldn't do for her.

Soon we started going to business net workings together and joined some associations also. We both were growing and discovering our abilities as powerful women business owners in Jacksonville.

Mrs. "B" was such an awesome lady, I looked up to her and learned a lot from her. I learned how to be more compassionate, how to listen more. She taught me what "true" love was too. I never met Mr. "B", as he had already gone home to be with God before I moved to Florida. When momma "B" talked about Mr. "B" I could feel the love she still had for him, even though he was gone. I never met him, but I know that the love they shared I could only hope to know true love like that one day.

During the rest of the year I helped her as a consultant, even when I found a job.

Time has gone by so quickly; it is already 1999 and I've been working for an elevator company in new construction. It's got my adrenaline going, I'm missing construction cleaning and thinking I may start the business soon. Keisha is graduating in June from high school and Kita is now a junior in college. Time waits for no one., I keep telling myself; if I'm going to start the business, I need to get busy.

SHE'S GROWING

In 2000 Mrs. "B" opened a second center. She separated the two by leaving the infants to 1-year olds in the first center and putting 2-year-olds to 12-year olds in the second center. I was so excited for her. She had been talking about retiring but she wasn't ready.

The new center is great, she's excited about its growth. She was especially excited about the fact she had been in business for five years. She once told our women's group about the time she applied for her first loan. She said the loan officer denied her the loan and told her that most small businesses fail in two years. When Mrs. "B" was ready to open the second center she went back to the bank. The same loan officer was still working there when she applied for the loan. This time she was approved but she didn't take the loan. She told the loan officer no thank you, she wasn't going to take the loan, she reminded the loan officer that he

denied her three years before and she just wanted
him to see she was still in business and growing.
She told the loan officer he shouldn't group
everyone the same, each individual person should
be treated as an individual. She told the loan officer
she was still in business and was about to open her
second center.

Mrs. "B" turned her daycare centers into one non-
profit center in 2001. She truly believed in caring
for children from low-income homes. She not only
cared for the children, but she also cared for their
parents. She was grandma to a lot of children,
everyone loved her. She did a lot in the community,
raised a lot of children. She also added free
"Volunteer Pre-Kindergarten" to the center. Mrs.
"B" was in her 70's and a pioneer, she worked hard
and loved all.

PEOPLE FOR A SEASON

You know, in life you meet people who have been
put in your life for various reasons. Mrs. "B" was
one of those people for me. She taught me true
servitude, and I later learned God let me come to
Florida to serve her. I didn't realize this until the
end of 2005. It dawned on me I had been serving
her for 6 years. I learned a lot too, most of all I
learned you can't be a good leader if you can't be a
good servant. I not only served Mrs. "B", but I
became another daughter to her. She was very
important to me, I could talk to her about anything,
vent and cry. She once told me when I was looking
to buy a house to ask God about it. Only buy what I

really want, what Cherron wanted. She was always telling me to stop living for everyone else and do something for me.

Mrs. "B" went home to be with God November 2006. I miss her, but I know she's watching over me.

N.O.K. COMES TO LIFE IN FLORIDA

Time has gone by so quickly; it is already 1999 and I've been working for a company in new construction. It's got my adrenaline going, I'm missing construction cleaning and thinking I may start the business soon. Keisha is graduating in June from high school, Kita is now a junior in college. I look at my daughters and I'm so glad I never became a quitter. Time waits for no one; I keep telling myself. If I'm going to start the business, I need to get busy.

It's August of 1999, I've gone to a meeting of a group called "Sisters In Business". It's a group of all African American Woman who own businesses or want to start one. I am now motivated to move into action.

It's September of 1999 and I've gotten things in place to start working the business. I've changed the "Ch" to a "K". People were having a hard time remembering to pronounce the "Ch" as a "K".

I'm marketing as inexpensively as I can. I'm trying to let the construction companies know I'm out here. Break through!!! I've been given my first contract. I worked with two other people, we finished, and the company is pleased with our work. I'm on my way. A few more contracts have come in but not enough to work totally for myself.

I'm still working a full-time job, started using "CC" because the accounting departments with the construction companies, knew Cherron worked for the elevator company. It's December, I have gotten information about a group I can join for construction companies and trades. I started taking some courses through Florida A & M University. After I finish the courses, it would put me in a bonding program. I'm learning a lot since my move to Florida. The move has really paid off for me so far, personally and for business. I know now to always ask God first.

God has told me this business is to give back and lead men to Him. Give jobs to the homeless, then He added ex-offenders. The mission is still to provide transportation and a meal while they are working. God has had to remind me on occasion, I can't be all things to all people. I can't hire everyone; everyone doesn't want to pick themselves up. Help only those who want to be helped.

Sometimes, when I can't see how to continue to service them like He has told me to, I remind Him He said for me to do this. I ask Him how, money is short, where is it to come from......................And just like that money comes from somewhere. He is AWESOME.

GOD SAYS IT'S TIME

April 17th, 2000, the Lord woke me up this morning saying resign today. I've been in dire need of new transportation, but He tells me he will not provide me with any more transportation to work out there.

I went into the office and trouble was waiting for me. I kept my head up and gave my resignation that morning. I was given the two weeks pay but told to leave that same day. I really and truly had to totally put myself in God's hands. Knowing how He works I knew He had me covered in every way.

June 28th, 2000, I had an abnormal pap smear and had to have a procedure done called "LEAP" done to see if there was a possibility that I might have cervical cancer cells. I remembered I was not alone; God was by my side. Waiting on the results was hard but I put my mind on other things. I contracted myself out to various places to work doing administrative work. My unemployment has been denied and my appeal was a no also. Now I'm really looking to God for answers. I cried to Him one night saying I was my family's only means of income, and He stopped me. He said He was tired of hearing me say that I had been saying it for years. He said let me show you who really has been taking care of you. It seemed as though the world stopped. I could get no work; I had no transportation and the small income I had coming in was just enough to pay for the house note. Every day, every week, I saw God work a miracle, make a way and show me who was really in charge.

HE'S MAKING A CHANGE

September 2000, my biopsy is negative, I'm okay and God is good. He has told me to make some changes to the company. I've asked Him to guide me and give me directions as to where to start and where to go. Everything comes in time, when it's supposed to, I'm learning a lot and really leaning on my Father in Heaven.

First, He tells me to get a new look for the company. I'm not sure what He means so I ask Him to clarify. At a luncheon I ran into a counselor of mine, who told me she finally has the brochure she has been working on. I had forgotten all about it, I made an appointment to meet with her the following week. At the luncheon God let's me know to make a difference, to have an edge with the business. Help me, I say. I decided to wait and see what this brochure looked like and would move on it.

Today is the day I'm meeting my counselor. I sat down in her office and she hands me the brochure. I'm really speechless, I look at her and can't believe its mine. Then when I can finally say something, I say, "I hope I can live up to this", she assures me I will. She then sets it up so that I can meet the person who did the brochure to work out a way to pay him. I'm excited and can't wait to get it out. Going home, God tells me to hand deliver each brochure. I said okay and got started. I took my brochure to every construction site with a job trailer I could find. Always left with a good feeling and the possibility of a contract.

The gentleman who did my brochure needed some help at the time. So, I bartered my administrative services to pay for my brochure. I worked three days to pay for my brochure and was going to leave; only for him to offer to pay me to come in three days a week and continue to work. I said okay, since Thanksgiving was coming up and I needed the extra money. He let me go the week before Thanksgiving and didn't give me my brochure on disk. He said there was nothing written saying he "had" to give me my brochure. I would have to come to him and pay for any changes I might need to make to my brochure. I left mad but chalked it up to a loss and lesson learned.

Thanksgiving has come and gone, Keisha is in Okinawa, she joined the Air Force. Kita couldn't stay long, she's a senior in college now and preparing for graduation. In praying this particular night, I said to God, "you know, I've been lying to You and to myself, I'm asking you for a husband, I don't want to be by myself anymore. I want someone who will give me emotional support and lift me up and encourage me. I want help raising my sons. Someone to share good and bad moments with. Someone who will be supportive to me and the mission you have me on".

Christmas is great, I just received my first large contract and it's also a state contract. The business is certified as a Minority Business Entity with the city and the state, so this is good. I'm excited and anxious. I've had to hire 10 people, and I also picked up a small janitorial contract that I can do myself one day a week: more income. God is making ways.

.....AND I THOUGHT HE WAS SENT BY GOD

It's the middle of January, once again, my wires
have gotten crossed. We started this big project, my
first state project. I've got an administrative
assistant working with me. Today is the first day of
payroll and my computer seems to have a virus or
something. It has been one of those weeks. A
gentleman caller has been pursuing me, I have no
time. I decided to go up to the church and get some
prayer from my prayer buddy. We talk for a while,
and we pray. I then tell her I have a computer
problem and need my computer looked at like
yesterday. She hands me a card and said call this
man, He works on the church's computers, and he
comes to my house as well. So, I took his card and
called. I got an appointment for the same day; I'll
meet him at 4:00pm.

Where has the time gone; it is 3:00, time to pick up
the children, payroll hasn't called yet, and the
computer man is coming at 4:00.

We have just arrived at the house, there is a truck
sitting in front of my house, my oldest son is
playing in the yard. I pull in the driveway and this
man gets out, I'm wondering who he is and what
does he want. He walks up the driveway and says
he's the man who has come to fix my computer. I
looked at him and thought, does he know what he's
doing? There is so much to be done right at this
point, get the children at the table to do homework;
call payroll and give the hours of employees; and
make sure this person doesn't make any more
problems for my computer. I let him in so he can

get started while on the phone to give payroll hours. After about 30 minutes I go out to my office to check on this person, he's doing things to my computer, I tell him to not charge me more than the $35 he said he would charge over the phone. I leave back out to help the children at the table. Fifteen more minutes pass I check on him again, he says the computer is alright, he would have to come back Saturday, to reinstall a program that was lost, he would do that at no charge. By 6:00pm the day is over, and I exhale.

IS THIS BUSINESS OR PLEASURE?

It's 9:00pm the children are down and I'm sitting down taking a load off my feet and mind, when the phone rings. I pick it up only to hear the computer man's voice at the other end, what does he want? He works a full-time job and does his computer business on the side part-time. He wants to know if he can just call and talk sometimes. I said yes, what was I thinking? We talked for two hours before I realized it. The conversation was pleasant and uplifting, he's quiet and shy. We say good night and he'll see me Saturday. At 11:30pm I get another call, it's the man who fixes my van, he wants to know if he can come by sometimes. I told him I not interested at this time, but he can call. I started wondering what's really going on. I don't need any distractions at this time, I want and need only to have God as the center of my attention at this time right now.

Saturday is here, the boys are on punishment, in timeout in their room. My daughter is watching movies with me, there is a knock at the door. It's him, I forgot he was coming. I let him in and go back to my movies. After about what seems like hours, I go out and check on him to see if I can help, we figure out that he's trying to install a program that is older than the one I had on my computer. I tell him not to worry about it I'll borrow the program from someone I know. Before I realize what's coming out of my mouth, I've invited him in to watch a movie and he said yes. After the movie we talked for a while. I start telling him how I have to take a crew of people to a job that's 50 minutes away. We had just started doing floors for the Juvenile Detention Center in St. Augustine. He volunteered to follow me and bring me back home so that I could leave the van with the supervisor. I thanked him and told him when to come back. I pack the kids and take them to a friend's house and go back home to wait until it's time to go. At 8:30 there's a knock on the door, I tell myself he's early, I open the door and it's the mechanic who fixed my van. I invite him in and tell him I'll be leaving shortly and where I was going. He starts yelling asking me why I took the contract, why couldn't it wait. He was saying all the wrong things, not once did he offer to help me out. I told him he had to leave. I just didn't need to hear what he was saying at that time. As he's leaving, the computer guy comes to the door ready to follow me; I introduce them and tell him I'm ready. He followed me while I picked up every worker and then took them to the job. He helped take the equipment inside the building and waited for me. I'm thinking to myself, why is he being so nice and why am I not feeling threatened or anything bad about being with this man. After everything and everybody is in place, I'm ready to go home. On the ride home we talk about everything. It's a great ride back and when we got to my house, we sat outside and talked for a little while longer. He is quite the gentleman. I don't have any ill feelings about being alone with him, it's nice.

GOD ANSWERS PRAYERS IN HIS OWN TIME

It's Tuesday morning and I'm getting ready to go pick up my administrative assistant for work. I start talking to God. Lord, you have me on this path to do your will. You taught me that I must believe in You for all things big and small. Please don't let my flesh be tempted and let me get off the path you have me on. My life has been so full of turmoil, and even though the good things have outweighed the bad things; I still wished things would have gone a little smoother for me at times.

That evening when we sat down to talk, he said to me he felt I was the woman he had asked God for. He had also prayed the year before for someone to come into his life. He said he believed God had brought us together. He asked me to marry him, and I said yes. He said he didn't want to set a date at that time, but it would be before the year was out. We prayed and asked God to guide us and direct our steps from that day forth. I thought God was first in his life, but he had me fooled. I truly learned what it meant to be able to "discern" those who are not Christians from the inside out.

CAN WE SURVIVE THE ATTACKS OF THE ENEMY?

It seemed after he asked me to marry him, the bottom dropped out. We were truly being tested. Everything from my sons getting in trouble at school, to losing employees and almost having to shut down my company. Money was not coming in on time. I could see no end in sight as to when the project would be finished or if I would be able to finish it. He was being very supportive; he helped out where he could. I had gotten to a point on the project where we worked evenings sometimes and some weekends; it left no time to try and have a relationship. Things seemed to be coming so fast. Kita was graduating from college Mother's Day weekend, Keisha was coming home for that, we had decided to look for a bigger house and when were we going to get married. Every time we decided on a date, something happened, and it didn't happen.

GOD CAN WORK IT OUT

Kita's graduation was great, Keisha's visit was wonderful. We found a house and he moved the little ones and me into the house Memorial Day weekend. I finished the project in the middle of June, I'm still in business, and I am now truly a sub-contractor. We got married on July 6, 2001 and he moved into the house July 9th. He is now a full-time entrepreneur just like I am, and we help each other out. We spend as much time as we can together, and we talk a lot. We laugh and I haven't

cried in a while. I used to be afraid to feel so
happy, but I've learned that's what we're here for;
to laugh and enjoy life since we don't know when
our journey will end. I keep God first, I consult
Him on everything, I follow His lead. I ask Him for
directions weekly and He reminds me that He is still
in control.

JUST WHEN I THOUGHT I HAD IT RIGHT
THIS TIME.....................

It's our first-year anniversary and we are arguing.
He asked me how did I expect him to know how to
be a husband after just one year. I told him, it's not
something you learn, it's something you feel from
the time you get married; from your heart. It was
things like this from time to time that made me
wonder what have I done.

How can a person seem like one thing during the
dating period but become a whole other person once
the wedding is over? He watched TV 24 hours; it
was worse than having to contend with another
woman. He was a hermit; he didn't care for
company at our home and he didn't want us leaving
too often. I eventually figured out that he wanted
children, but he didn't want a wife.

He left me in February 2003. When I realized I had
been paying the bulk of the bills, I refused to give
him a check for the rent for February. He told me I
wasn't average or normal. Didn't he notice that
when we met, I wore a pink hard hat and steel toed
shoes. I ran a crew of men and was coming home
dusty from head to toe, often. When he left, bills

were due. A company I was using in Boca Roton, Florida was factoring my invoices (paying me in advance for my receivables), refused to release money I had in an account they held; so, I could not make payroll. When we rented the house, my credit was not good enough to put me on the lease next to him, so the lease was in his name with me and the children listed as living in there with him. The Saturday he moved out, Joe had a program at church, so the children and I left for church while he moved. After the program was over, I heard the Holy Spirit say call the rental office to see why he told them he was moving. I called and was told he was able to move and not be responsible for February's rent because he gave notice before the 5th of the month. I asked the lady on the phone did he tell her my children and I weren't moving and that we were still in the house. She stated he had not told her that and the house was going up for rent on Monday. She told me to fax her a letter stating we were still in the house, and I would have to go through my own credit check in order to stay in it. I got some paper and wrote a letter and faxed it from the church. Then I prayed and let God know it was in His hands since I didn't pass the first credit check.

Monday afternoon I received a call from the property management office. I was told they received the letter, and I needed to come in and sign a new lease. I informed them I was on the way to school to pick up a sick child but could come the next day. The lady on the phone said that would be fine, anytime by Friday would be good.
Tuesday morning, I got up, did my devotional time and heard the Holy Spirit say, be at the rental office

by 9:00am when they open. I dropped everyone off to school and was there at 9:00. I told the lady behind the counter who I was and what I was there for. She smiled and said, "we have everything ready for you, you know this is a twelve-month lease, right?" I said "yes" and signed the lease. It had just myself and my three little ones listed on it. I got in my car and crying thanked God. He is so awesome, he truly showed me He can and will make a way out of no way.

SHUTTING IT DOWN

I've decided to shut the business down. I was tired of people looking to me for what they needed and things working so against me most of the time.

The day I made this decision I was headed for a meeting. While on the way, I told Kita I had decided to shut down the business and asked her what she thought about it. She said most people when they shut down their businesses it's because they no longer liked what they did. I thought about that, and it was not the case at all for me, I loved the work, I enjoyed the people. This really made me think. I had helped many people transition out of shelters. Woman got their children back into their care working for No Ordinary Kleaning. No, I definitely had not stopped enjoying what I did. I planted many seeds in people and definitely didn't want to stop doing that. After all, my business is my ministry, to help those who are down and to lead them to God. What really bothered me more than anything was not having the working capital I needed and not being able to make payroll on time all the time.

YOU'RE THE ONE WHO HOLDS US TOGETHER

I got to the place where the meeting was being held and ran into two of my business associates, both in construction. I told them I was closing my business; I was tired. At the same time, they said, "You can't do that". Then one of them said to me, "They needed, me because I was so helpful to them as well as others. Whenever they need some information about something, they can always come to me for it. I was the reason they were hanging in there with their businesses." I told them thank you and I would think about what they said and would be in touch.

The Beaver Street Enterprise Center (an incubator for small businesses) was being built. It was to house small businesses at below cost for office rental space to help them grow and move on. It would include office space, furniture, phones, computers, internet, a receptionist and resources to help us become better business owners. I had been approached to go in it but wasn't sure if I was ready to move my business out of my home. The only thing holding up the process and decision for me was my giving them my business plan. That morning when I was getting ready to leave the house the Holy Spirit told me to take my business plan with me to the meeting. It didn't call for me to bring one to the meeting, but I was obedient and took it with me.
When I got to the training room for the workshop, I saw a gentleman that was on the board for the

Beaver Street Enterprise Center. He worked for Fresh Ministries, a Faith Based Organization that was really working on making a difference in neighborhoods in Jacksonville. He approached me and asked when was I going to get that business plan to him. I gave him the one I had on me. He turned out to be a very good person who was in my life for a "season". He became my mentor and showed me a lot. He too has gone on to be with the Lord, I miss him but will keep with me always what I learned from him.

The next month (March) I saw a vision of me in the choir at church. I thought, I must be losing my mind, that can't be for me to do. I was an usher at church and wanted to teach Sunday school. Joining the choir had never crossed my mind. Secretly, we all sing, some in the shower, some while cooking, some while cleaning, but it's just for us. Some of us really do make a joyful "noise" for the Lord, but we don't want to do that in front of a crowd of people. A few days later I saw it again and said to God, "please don't make me do this". The next time there was choir rehearsal I showed up, I was placed in the alto section. I felt there were some individuals who didn't want me there, but I was doing this unto the Lord. I later found out God had me do this because He wanted me to remember to praise Him at all times; no matter what is going on. At this time in my life I felt like a hurricane and a tornado had collided with me struggling to get out from between them. Remember to never let your situation define you.

"CHANGING ME"

I called a friend of mine to check on her and see how she was doing. She was one of my sisters in business and a lot of us were having problems with our business at the time. I told her my husband had left me two months ago and to my surprise she said, "good". Shocked that she would say such a thing; I said, "what did you say?" She said, "stop always trying to help everybody out. Let someone pursue you the next time." We talked about our children, and our business and made a date for lunch.

I got off the phone and thought about what she said, and she was right. All three husbands were men who I had picked up, brushed off, built their self esteems, motivated them to feel they could conquer the world. When they left, they took what I taught them and gave themselves to someone else. I decided to sit back and do some self-evaluating. I realized I needed to stop dealing with "needy" men. I owned up to the fact that I had a hidden agenda each time I married, so I knew why the marriages had not worked. I needed to work on me, make some changes so that I had a whole new way of thinking and handling me. Thank goodness for "real" friends, who will be honest with you for your sake.

In April I received a phone call telling me I had been approved for office space in the Beaver Street Enterprise Center. I would be one of the first tenants when it opened in June. I talked to God and told Him, up to this time, I only saw my business as a means to feed my family. I needed to change my way of thinking, or I would never be able to move ahead and take my business to another level. In three weeks, I saw myself doing a million dollars in business, I was excited. I moved in my office June 2, 2003. The media was there, I was one of three new tenants, we signed our leases together while being photographed. We were interviewed and asked about our businesses, that day I received all kinds of marketing and advertising that I could never have been able to pay for at that time. About 5:00 I saw I had received a call from my sister in Georgia. I was excited to tell her about my day, she had Joc and Aaron in Georgia with her, so I called to speak to everyone. Barbara informed me that our oldest brother had passed while on vacation in Jamaica. She said I needed to come home as soon as I could, they were waiting for his body and his wife to return so we could have a funeral for him. Talk about an emotional roller coaster. The morning was full of excitement for me, with more media attention than I ever dreamed of then the evening was full of hurt over the loss of my brother. Barbara told me she would let me know when to come home, the children were alright but taking it hard.

LET GO AND LET GOD

September is here, its been a hectic year but I'm still standing. I have bid on four or five large projects. I decided it was all in God's hands. His timing was everything. Most of the year I had a small janitorial contract working for me, with three people working it. I was barely making it. October rolled around and I received three of the projects I had bid on. I had two weeks to train and get certified by OSHA (Occupational Safety & Health Administration) in construction. God made a way for me to train sixty-two homeless people and hire 45 of them. My gross sales shot up to $145,000 in two and a half months to end the year. I know the God I serve can make the impossible possible.

I want to say thank you to my brother, Alfred and my sister-in-law, Maddie, they let Joc and I come and stay with them. I was waiting on my place to become available to move into at the beginning of 2004. It was very interesting living with them because we realized we had four generations of people living there. I'm a "Baby Boomer", Tony and Monique are "Generation X, our daughters are "Generation Y" and their son is "Generation Z". Sometimes it was interesting, as I may say something about a television show that they never saw because they were too young to see it. Sometimes the girls would say something that I didn't have a clue about since I don't keep up with trends. Their son just didn't have a clue about too much of anything, it made us realize that it is important to know as much as we can about what is going on around us so that we can be "in the loop". Our younger generations have so much going on these days, yet they don't know too much about our history and why and how things can be like they are today. We need to make sure we share with each generation and learn more ourselves so that we can all have much information about the past, the present and the future. Most of the time they were laughing at me because most of it sounds foreign to me. Thank goodness I have a 16 year who doesn't mind explaining things too me that comes from her generation. It's important that "Generation Z" knows our Black History. My nephew, who was 7 at the time thought I used to be a slave, because I had often used the phrase "I been working like a slave". Boy, do we have to watch what we say and never think yourself too "big" or too much of an "adult" to answer a question from a little person. Never thought I'd feel "old", until one day, in 1987, my little sister asked me did they have telephones back in my day. (kids; smile) Thank you to the Butler family for the laughter, the lessons from the various generations and most of all for the love. You talk about blended families, we really lived together in what seemed like a bubble of our own. It makes you feel good when you can live in "peace and harmony" with a whole other family and not have any discord amongst yourselves.

MY PEOPLE PERISH FOR LACK OF KNOWLEDGE.................

We worked until March 2004. We picked up another large project for the City of Jacksonville. You know when God gives you a God sized task, you have to make sure you stay on track and follow "His" lead and not take over the lead.

Things were going so well for me that when I got a call from a business associate, I thought I should help her. She also owned a business in the Beaver Street Enterprise Center. She told me she, her husband and her two children, needed a place to stay for the night and could I put them up. I was still in the house since my husband left me and had no one at home but the two children and my grandson. There are only two children because I had given my oldest son back to his "birth" family. At 14 he decided he wanted to get to know them. I told him he had to choose but he would not go back and forth between the two families. He was already giving me problems and doing nothing in school. I gave him to his birth mother's sister in August of 2004.

I was skeptical but having talked with her at the office and believing she was truly "walking with God" I let them come and stay. As old as I was, I still acted naïve. A few days turned into months, and they didn't offer a dime. I told them if they couldn't help pay the rent, they could give me $150 on food every month; as her husband was on disability. They gave me the first $50 after staying two months and said it was hard to give the $150. She said business wasn't doing well. In May they left for Myrtle Beach for their anniversary, I thought it strange since they had no money to give me for staying. When they returned, I sat them down and told them what the household bills were, and that I expected them to pay half from this point on or they would have to move the first of June. The week before they moved out, she bought a "new" Ford SUV. They moved the following week and acted as though I shouldn't expect them to pay me anything for the months they stayed. She even stopped speaking to me and joined in with another female business owner in the building who had a problem with me. God protected me from the things they tried to do to make things bad for me. He also showed me Proverbs 6:1-5; which tells us the needy, orphans and widows will always be around for us to help. But we can only help if we have the means to do so. We can't help people putting ourselves out and expecting God to help us out of a bind we put ourselves in.

2004 was going okay, could have been better. In July I went up to Georgia to some meetings and to bid on two janitorial contracts; one was with the federal government and one with the state government. I drove my company truck up, with no intention to stay longer than two days as I had to be in Orlando to receive an award that week. I did my walk through for both contracts and was about to leave when my van wouldn't start. To ward off the anxiety attack that was trying to come on, I started thinking about what I could do to get back to Florida. I decided to catch the Greyhound bus, an express would get me there by 3:00am in the morning. I made a call to Florida and asked a friend if she would take me to Orlando and she said I could use her truck and take myself. I got on the bus and prayed telling God I didn't understand why this was happening, but I knew He was in control. I started to take out some work and start working on my numbers for one of the bids, when the Holy Spirit said, "just sit back, close your eyes and rest. I did just that and slept most of the time while heading home. When I arrived in Florida, I called the person whose truck I was going to borrow and then caught a cab to her house. I went home, showered, packed and left for Orlando.

ME, HONORED.........FOR WHAT?

On the ride to Orlando, I realized had I driven home from Georgia, I would have gone into my office at 2:00am in the morning, got on the computer, then went home, showered, packed and left for Orlando. I could have killed myself, not having gotten any sleep. Thank you, Lord.

The conference is interesting. I had to be here because I was receiving an award. Several people are here, other business owners I know and some I have yet to meet. The awards banquet is in the evening, it's a formal dinner. I feel like a queen. I love dressing up and looking pretty. Especially being in construction, people tend to wonder if you can dress and carry yourself as a lady. Yes, I can and enjoy it. Everyone looked so nice, it was fun.

I've just received an award from the Florida Minority Supplier Diversity Council for "Supplier of the Year" 2003 for hiring 45 homeless people and putting them to work on three major construction projects. I felt like a star, receiving an Emmy award. Being honored for something you see as just the right thing to do, because you want to help people brings rewards from heaven that you could never imagine.

WHAT IS UP?????????

It's September, the van was fixed, and I went to Georgia to pick it up. Halfway home it broke down on me again. I called the mechanic who fixed it and he came and got it and I called someone at home to come and get me. I was so distraught; I told God I was staying in the house until I heard from Him. What was I to do?

By this time Aaron is now with their birth family also. He just would not behave in school, and it had become a real problem for me. God told me to give him back to the birth family, but it was really hard for me. I was the only "mommy" he knew. He didn't know the birth family at all. I cried and told God I didn't understand why He wanted me to give up my baby boy. He told me if I didn't, my son would keep my life in constant turmoil. So, I signed him over to his grandmother. So now it's only Joc and I.

From Sunday to Tuesday, I fasted and prayed and cried. I prayed in the closet, and I slept in the closet at times. I figured if I was to pray in secret in the closet, if I slept in there, I wouldn't miss the answer. I thought back to everything that had been going on, having to move out of the house I lived in when my husband left me, moving into an area I was not crazy about living in. It dawned on me I was in Egypt; I wanted to get back to Caanan. By Wednesday, I had to leave the house to check on a contract, I got a ride, took care of the problem and asked the person to leave me downtown by the water. I sat and let the water calm me and then headed for the bus stop. When I got home and put my key in the door, it dawned on me that if I didn't make some serious changes in my life, I would never get past where I was at that time. I realized no matter how hard I worked, how well the business did I would have nothing if I didn't make some changes to me, in my mind and in my roots.

IN THE PRESENCE OF MY ENEMIES………..

Thursday morning, I got up and had this feeling something good was going to happen to me today. I did my hair, put on makeup and wore a dress to the office; I never wore dresses to work. I don't know why I did this, but it was for a reason. I felt as if someone else was getting me ready for work. Thank God for good project managers, he had taken care of the office while I was out of town and in the closet at home. The company was still standing.

About 11:00 I received a call from one of the women in the building who did not speak to me; I considered her an enemy. She asked me if I was going to the Minority Economic Development Week (MED Week) luncheon. I told her I didn't et a ticket in time, so I wasn't going. She then told me in my absence a representative from the local transportation entity in the city had left her a ticket for me to sit at their table. I told her I still could not go because I wasn't driving. She said I could ride with her and someone else who was going and for me to meet her in the lobby.

That other person turned out to be the woman who had lived at my house. I said a prayer and told God I didn't know what He was up to, but there was a reason for me to go to this luncheon, so I was going. I had to keep reminding myself of Proverbs 3:5-6 and lean not to "my" own understanding.

I got in her SUV with the two of them, still praying and telling God I knew I had been changed. I was with two people I wouldn't go across the street with let alone drive over to another side of town.

I had had such an ordeal in the past week and a half with the van I forgot I was on the board that was putting on the MED Week luncheon. That wasn't all I forgot……………………………..

While we were signing in the President of the board came up to me at the table and asked if I was signed in. Then she told me to come with her. As I was walking with her, she told me the board was sitting at the head table with the speaker. This table was on a platform looking out at everyone else seated in the room. We ran into the Vice President, who stopped us to remind me of the speech I had to give. I told her I couldn't, she reminded me she was writing the speech for me and it was already at my place at the table. I left them to go to the lady's room. I had tears welling up and needed to get my composure together. My mind was whirling, God was trying to tell me something. I got myself together and headed back to the room where the luncheon was being attended.

I got to my place setting only to realize I was sitting next to our guest speaker, Mr. Melvin Gravely. Mr. Gravely is the author of "The Lost Art of Entrepreneurship" and "Black and White Make Green", two very fascinating books. I was to speak before him. He and I talked and exchanged autographed copies of our books. The first time I published this book myself. I thought if Paul

Lawrence Dunbar could publish his book and sell it himself then so could I.

After the luncheon was over, I was able to tell the two women I had come with I had another way back to the office and thank you. It dawned on me at the end of the day, God let me live Psalm 23 all week long. The end of the week was awesome, and He truly comforted me with His rod and staff; as well as prepared a table for me in the presence of my enemies.

GOD'S GOT JOKES!!!!!!!!

I got back to the office and felt the need to call a minister I knew to have him pray for my business. I told him what had been happening with the van and the business and he began to pray. I expected him to ask God to send me people to work, working capital and contracts for the business. Instead, he asked God to bless me, to give me guidance and he started telling me how God was going to bless me with a man like Boaz (Ruth 2:5). He ended the praying telling me to continue "gleaning the fields" (Ruth 2:6-9). When he finished, I told him I was mad at him, I didn't ask him to pray for another husband for me. As far as I was concerned, I was a 'widow to marriage'. I asked him why he prayed that, and he said as a man of God he prayed as he was directed to do so by the Holy Spirit. I told him because of that I would take back being mad at him, but I didn't like it. At home that evening I looked up Boaz's profile and the word 'gleaning'. Christmas was nice for Joc and I, my oldest brother and his wife flew us up to Maryland to have Christmas with them. It was nice, Joc got to meet two of her great-great aunts on the Covington side, as well as some cousins. She's always wondered about family, since she only knows an aunt and uncle and talks to her father's mother on his side.

THE 11:59TH HOUR.................

Construction final clean is really where my heart is. We were working on a job on the Northside of town, and I had to stop and go get some window cleaner and lunch for my workers. I took a young lady with me who had been there since early morning. On the way I was stopped by the police because my tag was in the window of my van and not where it was supposed to be. I explained to the officer I didn't want it to be stolen as I had just gotten this tag for this van. The officer took my license to run it and write me a ticket. The other officer came up on the other side of the van and scared the young lady with me. He asked her what her name was, and she gave him the wrong name. She later told me she knew she had a warrant out for her arrest. When they saw she had given false information, she was told to get into the police car. The officer writing me the ticket came back to my van, had me sign my ticket and told me I could leave. I didn't want to leave her alone with that other officer, so while they looked up her real name I waited. The first officer came back to my van and told me she did have a warrant and she was going to have to go with them downtown. Then he said I had a warrant too and would also have to go downtown. He was nice enough to let me call my brother to come get my van. I then called my Administrative Assistant and told her where I had hidden some money in the van; she was to use it to bond me out. We went downtown only to find out I had a return check charge against me. While waiting for the officers to come back to the car (they went inside to pick up the warrants). I lead the young lady to the Lord; she accepted Jesus Christ as her Savior and told me she was not afraid of going into the jail.

After we were processed in, we were put in a cell block in time for dinner. It was not very tasty, since I wasn't hungry, I gave most of it away. After dinner I called Merisa from a pay phone, she could accept collect calls. She helps me a great deal, she not only called my brother for me with messages, she also allowed me to just talk to her. I found out I had to spend the night because it was my first time ever in there and I had to go before a judge the next day.

I sat at a table and started talking to some of the other women. I found out two other ladies were stopped on the corner of the same two streets I was stopped at and also had the same charges I had. I prayed with some of the ladies, told bible stories and had bible study before we had to turn in for the night. I now have a bit of an idea as to how Paul and Silas felt when they were locked up. The difference between me and them though, I wasn't beat and even though I prayed and talked about the bible, I couldn't get the jail doors to unlock (smile).

The next morning, while waiting to go before the judge, someone asked for prayer. They wanted a prayer said asking God to let everyone in the room we were in go get to go home that day. I said the prayer and when I was done another lady started us on a hymn. We were singing when they came to get us for the court room; we still didn't unlock those doors. I was given bail and was picked up by the bails bond company two hours later. On the way to her office, the bails bond lady asked me if I was okay, did it frighten me. I told her I lead someone to the Lord, prayed for some and had Bible study, I had the best time. She said she had never heard anyone say they had a good time while being locked up. She said that was good and God was good. I said, "Amen to that."

STAY IN GOD'S WILL.............................

2005 quietly ushered itself in. Be careful who you listen to, some people "act" like they're looking out for you, but it's themselves they're really helping.

Listening to other people I decided to chase janitorial contracts only. I didn't bid on any construction final cleaning in the beginning of the year. I was bidding military bases and homeland security contracts. Contracts that required a felony background check, not thinking about the fact my homeless people wouldn't be able to work these jobs.

It's April I have just gotten word I was being awarded a large janitorial contract with another city entity. I was excited because I met all the criteria they had asked for and felt I had truly gotten this contract on my own merit and with God. The homeless people I usually hired couldn't pass the background check, so I started hiring that "better caliber" of people others kept telling me I needed to hire. Half of them couldn't pass the background check either. The half that did pass, turned out to be individuals who had a plan to do me in.

The contract started out well, I was being pleasing to the customer. Then little by little things started going wrong. I eventually came to see that sometimes-large businesses make it look like they're trying to do right by and with small businesses. When all the time it's their 'hidden agenda' to make it look like we can't handle the work put before us. I wasn't the only small business going through this with this particular city entity. We helped each other grin and bear.

By September things had gotten to me so, I called the pastor that had prayed for me in September 2004. He told me the enemy was busy and was trying to distract me so I would miss an opportunity with God. He told me to read first and second Peter and don't make any major decisions for seven days, God had a profound message for me. This particular day I had to fire someone, so I called him back and asked him was that a major decision. He told me that he was working, to keep working but don't go buy a new van or house, apply for any loans, etc. So, I did what he said, I read the books over and over, I studied notes for those two books. Out of five vans I was down to one. This wasn't good since I provided transportation for my employees. On the ninth day, I called him again. I told him I had not yet heard from God and didn't understand. He told me again, to not make any major decisions and to read the book of James. He said it wasn't about the business; it was about me. He said God wanted me to pray more, study (not just read) and meditate on God's word more. I learned meditating meant listening to God's word preached by someone and listening to it over and over.

The next morning, I got up and prayed and read my bible and cut on Kenneth Copeland. I watched him every morning to start my day. When the broadcast was finished, Kenneth Copeland offered for "free" the entire CD set of his Great Lakes Prosperity Convention that had been in August. I called right away to have it sent to me.

Thursday, October 6 was to be pay day for my employees. The city entity I had been working for had been letting me invoice them every two weeks and paying me every two weeks. By this time, I was sick of the purchasing agent, and he was sick of me. Well, his office decided they would enforce the contract and told me they had up to thirty days to pay me. Six days out of the month we cleaned the terminal where the cruise ships came in, one was coming in on Saturday. I had been sick for a few days and was just too drained to deal with the mess that was going on. It was Friday morning, and I got a call saying none of my workers had showed up for work. I told the purchasing agent that they weren't coming since they didn't get paid the day before. He said he would put some people out there and charge me, I told him to do what he had to do and hung up. I laid on my sofa unable to function because I felt so bad and took a nap. My phone rang and I looked to see who was calling before picking up; it was the purchasing agent. I put the phone down and went back to sleep. About 1:30 I got up, ate and decided to listen to my messages. The purchasing agent left a message asking me to call with my bank account number and they would wire me the check they owed me so I could make payroll. I didn't call him back. He realized I would have no workers out at the terminal on that Saturday and wanted my people out there instead of people who didn't know what to do. I didn't call him back and went back to resting so I could be better by Monday.

Monday, October 10, 2005, I get a call from the purchasing agent asking me what did I want to do about the contract. I told him to resend it (cancel it). Sometimes it's not always about the money, sometimes it's just about 'peace of mind' and your integrity. I learned some people who are in place to help you as a small business aren't always on your side either. I had someone working for the city tell me I couldn't be a business and charitable too, because I hired the homeless. I was told I wasn't going to make it and I was handed a list of job openings. I left that person's office, got in my car and prayed. I told God I knew He had given me this business and I knew He would make it what it was supposed to be.

IT'S A NEW YEAR AND GOD IS TRULY IN CONTROL

I decided to take this time and do what God had instructed me to do. I got into Him and His word. I would start at 5:00am reading and studying myself and then turn on the television at 6:00am and started watching and listening to Kenneth Copeland and everyone else that came on after that. By the end of February, I lost my van, since I had no transportation, I had to let go of my temporary assignment and a small contract that I was doing. I really got into studying and meditating to the point I was so engulfed into what I was doing I would forget to eat. In March all my phones were disconnected, God really wanted my undivided attention. I learned my first step was to go to God and not just confess my sins but own up to what I was responsible for. What I had caused to happened in my life and for where I was responsible for at that time. When you go to God and say to Him, "I know this is my fault because I did.......................... and I'm asking you to forgive me and help me change my way of doing things. Help me get into Your will and on the path, You have for me. Then ask God not "why you" but "where do you go from this point?" Learn to forgive yourself, you can't go forward if you allow satan to keep reminding you of your past mistakes. As time went on, I got closer and closer to God. He started showing me things, He gave me Proverbs 8:33-35. He let me know I was afraid of wealth and that was why my finances could go no farther than they had. He let me know that I was not ready for what He had for me, because I would not be able to handle it. See God wants to give us all the desires of our hearts, but what you do with the little He gives you shows Him what you will do with bigger things He wants to give you. You must also remember God loves a cheerful giver; we must remember God wants to bless us to "be a blessing". I realized my childhood way of seeing money was messed up and what I saw made me a "spender". I asked God to change those roots, give me new roots so that I could handle my money better, and learn to give from my overflow and not give to the point I put myself in a bind. I read this book titled "Secrets of the Millionaire Mind" by T. Harv Eckerd. It helped me see the difference in being rich and being poor, what the thoughts were of people in those two categories were. I asked God to change those roots and give me new roots, I wanted what He had for me. I wanted to be able to handle it and I wanted to be a blessing to others His way.

Soon God started showing me things He had for me. He gave me scriptures like Mark 9:23 and reminding me of Mark 11:24. I was getting excited. In getting closer to God, I became more of a servant. Even though things had fallen down around me, and I saw no end in sight; I helped people where I could, sharing God's word, giving my testimonies, sharing what God had taught me up to that time. My compassion for people changed. I no longer wanted to just help people because I knew it was what God wanted. I helped people because I wanted them to know the goodness of God like I had truly come to know Him, from the inside out.

Even though to the physical eye it looked as if all was lost for me, I was so at peace within. By this time, I have been evicted from my townhouse and have had to move in with my oldest daughter. I'm not comfortable with this, but God has told me I'm not a good receiver. Even "rich" people are good receivers. So, I'm waiting, still studying and trying to grasp being a "good receiver". The more God showed me and talked to me about what He was doing for me, the more excited I got.

Forgiveness, we must forgive, or this can <u>hold</u> up everything.

It's two weeks before Christmas, I'm in church and the Holy Spirit has me go to the alter and pray for two men who are widowers. He then tells me to give them both a message to pray more, meditate on His words more, and study His words more. I was obedient but wondered what these men would think when I gave them these messages. I had to write one, he lived in another part of the state. The other I was able to call as I had met him when I joined a club, we belonged to in February earlier in the year; plus, he had called me on the Friday before, so I had a number for him. I am going home to Georgia to see my family. I can't wait, it's been two years since I was last up there. I need a hug from my mom and dad, and some relaxation, relate and release time with my sister.

MORE THAN "JUST" FRIENDS

Shadrach, Meshach, Abednego and Daniel. These four guys stuck together and stood on God's word like no one else. They trusted and believed God to bring them through the situations they were facing, while in captivity. Sometimes we can be in captivity in our minds, jobs, with people; whatever your "captivity", you must stand on God's word without doubt. He will see you through.

This is how I refer to myself and the three women that prayed, fasted, helped me out and saw me through the worst of what I was going through. They didn't stop calling me or drop out of sight like what I was going through would rub off on them. They encouraged me, they cried with me and for me. Even though they looked at what was happening in the natural, they believed God had something so big for me they wanted me to get through it.

We fed off each other spiritually day to day. Sometimes as you are going through the fire, others around you may also be going through and/or learning and receiving from your experience. God would give one of us a scripture for another, or we would have a revelation one for another; it was awesome to see it all unraveling. It wasn't easy but we knew since God is who He is we would come out smelling like roses. I was going through the hardest, but we each had something pressing we were dealing with.

God is so awesome; we each begin to be blessed in little ways. Through all of this we each arrived at a new spiritual level and we are still best buds. We also watched those who came in contact with us be blessed.................Awesome.

I learned sometimes we go through for the benefits of others. People are always watching you to see how you react and handle situations that come your way. I would ask God whoever was watching, had they gotten the message yet? Could a sista' get a break. (smile) The best part is to "not" look like what you are going through or what you've been through. I never looked like I was homeless, jobless or careless in all of this. No one new except those very close to me. The stronger I got spiritually, the more beautiful I became from the "inside out". I felt like a new person, I talked like a new person, I functioned like a new person.

A friend of mine, Debbie, of Debbie's Doghouse, the Hotdog Lady on Lane Avenue in Jacksonville, FL, quoted something Mother Theresa once said. For me, I always felt God was giving me my share and having me carry some of the burden of someone else not as strong as I, once heard a sermon on pertaining to that one day. But this is what Mother Theresa said, "I know God won't give me more than I can bear............. Sometimes I just wish he didn't trust me so much." When she quoted that to me, it dawned on me that was the way I felt. I sometimes wish God didn't trust me to handle so much.

To my friends, I want to say many thanks to you and may God really bless you exceedingly, abundantly, above all you could ask or imagine.

Shadrach – M. R.   Meshach – A. B.
         Abednego – G. Y.
                  And me .... Daniel

BOAZ HAS ARRIVED??????????

I am on my way home to Georgia to have Christmas
with my sister. I am driving, it's late, Joc is asleep
and I'm listening to a CD. Suddenly I started to
cry, and I ask myself what is wrong with you. This
song has me thinking about him, why? He isn't
interested in me like that and I'm in no position at
this time, technically homeless, having a job
working one day a week and no transportation of
my own. I didn't want to get involved with anyone
at this time, I felt I must wait until things changed
for me and were better. I must be able to pull my
weight and help myself. I played that song again
and again and kept seeing him in my mind. I knew
I had fallen in love with him, and no one knew but
me and God. I felt like I was in a desert wanting
someone who seemed like just a mirage at this time.
I got to Georgia safely and dropped it. Christmas
was so nice; I got to spend time with my family in
Georgia and I got my hug from my mom and dad.
It was great.

Boaz, according to the profile in my Application
Study Bible, was a man of his word, sensitive to
those in need, caring for his workers. It also said he
had a keen sense of responsibility and integrity, and
he was a successful and shred businessman. I really
saw all these features in this person before I got to
know him and even more after I started paying him
more attention.

He is one of the widowers I was to pray for, he was
the one who was the local call. I called him to give
him the message. I started off saying to him, "I

don't know you or anything about you, other than what you told me on Friday. I called to let you know God has a message for you. He wants you to place the importance you had on your wife on Him now. He wants you to pray more, meditate and study His word more." He said okay and thank you for the message. A few minutes later he called me back and asked if he could talk with me about some things that were going on with him at the time as he had no one else to talk with. What he talked about was a modern-day situation of David and Saul. He truly has a calling on his life, and he is going to go far. The next day he called me again, three days later he was still calling and let me know he felt he needed to talk to me every day.

I would see him at our monthly meetings, but I was not interested in anyone at this time. As far as I was concerned, I was not in a position to become involved with anyone. I didn't even want to be "bothered" with a man. It's amazing how you feel you should keep yourself to yourself until things get "better". It's funny how God works, He always has another plan. In the past I had always helped out the men in my life. This time God showed me I didn't have to help him out, he was truly a "real" man and didn't need me to define himself. I wasn't in a position to do anything for him in any way but let him pursue me and pursue me he did.

In studying the book of Ruth, I learned the book wasn't so much about Boaz taking Ruth out of her bad financial situation. The gist of the book was about the relationship that developed between Boaz, Ruth and Naomi. God wants us to love and respect the people He brings into our lives. We must make sure we don't let our circumstances make us miss the opportunity for love, strength and resources that we are given in our present relationships. I later realized God was testing and preparing me for what He was about to do for me.

Earlier in February of 2006, while driving, I just started thanking God for all He had taught me, showed me and for where He had brought me from. From the projects in SE Washington, DC to the Congressional Black Caucus and its events, to Kansas and learning the art of socializing and entertaining. Also, to know how to talk to people from everywhere and to be no respecter of persons. I realized I was starting to accept the fact that God had this Boaz for me, I started saying to myself, who ever he was he was someone in the political ring.

I really believed he was the Boaz God had revealed to me in 2004. Our relationship just flows. We seem so in sync and there is a very strong relationship developing between him, myself and Joc. We laugh a lot and talk about everything. I believe I have that "true" love with him, I learned about from Mrs. "B". **NOTE**: I later learned when God gives you a person, place or thing, you don't have to "believe" He sent it, you don't have to "think" He sent it, you don't have to "figure it out", wondering if he sent it, YOU WILL "KNOW" He sent it.

I pray that those who read this book will see if you let God lead you and be obedient to what He tells you do; He will keep you and give you peace.

Remember, you have to be a good servant before you can be an effective leader.

I just want to say, seek God first and He will give you the desires of your heart. Don't be selfish in your desires and always help others where you can. Sometimes the simplest things can mean more to someone than any pot of silver or gold. God is good and He wants us to prosper, but we must not let the material riches of the world take His place. We must be just as rich spiritually as we can be materially, remember 3 John 1:2. I thank God for my Pastor at my church at First Timothy Baptist Church and my church family since I've been living in Florida. I thank God for my life, as I've come to learn God doesn't put more on you than you can bear. Once you realize God has a calling on your life and you accept the call you must let Him have His way with you. Let Him lead, while you be obedient to what He tells you to do. He will open doors and windows where you thought there were chains and locks. He will weed out the people in your life that will hinder your progress towards His mission for you. God will make your enemies help you, when they have set out to hurt you. God will place people in your path, sometimes if only for a brief moment, to get you further along in your journey. Watch, listen and do what God commands of you, even when it makes no sense. Remember: "Lean not to your own understanding" (Proverbs 3:5); "Worry not about tomorrow" (Matt 6:25-33); "Wait on God" (Psalms 27:14); "Be not afraid, for God is always with you" (Psalms 91:10-11).

Special thanks go out to:

>My pastor, Rev. Frederick
Newbill, Sr.
Mrs. Pam Newbill
Mrs. Loretta Hagen
Derick & Gail Young
Mrs. Doretha Smith
Mr. & Mrs. Paul Roberts
Mark & Diane Deas
Sandra Cody
Patrica Clark
Dorothy Carter
Wayne & Carol Clark

Those people were my church family
at First Timothy Baptist Church, for nine years
Who always had an
encouraging word or something nice to
say, not knowing
what was really going on
with me.

GOD BLESS THEM ALL!!!

JUST FOR YOU!!!!!!!!!

Ladies remember to always feed the woman in you. Don't look for a man to feed it, you start. So that when you are with the man you want to be with you can tell him what your "woman" wants, and needs are. Buy lingerie for you, give yourself candlelight bubble baths, take yourself out for ice cream.

"RELEASE NEGATIVE ENERGY FRIDAY"!!!!!

I created this for myself when I moved to Florida with the three little ones by myself. On Fridays, they got fed and put to bed by 8:00pm. I told them I was not their momma unless they were bleeding to death or dying. This time I took for myself, I would treat myself to dinner and a movie. After about 4:00pm, I stopped listening to any drama, take any drama calls and didn't have any unwanted or uninvited guests invade or try to ruin my time for me. I wouldn't let anyone or anything in my space that was going to try and take up my time with foolishness, in my time put aside just for me. I would go to Red Lobsters, Bennigan's, Applebee's, or whatever I have a taste for that evening. I would rent me two movies (comedy or action; nothing to create any kind of pity party) and I would have my dinner and a movie and a nice glass of Chardonnay with orange juice and enjoy myself.

NOTES:

What Do You Do To Laugh To Keep From Crying??

_____
_____
_____
_____
_____
_____
_____
_____
_____

_____
_____
_____
_____
_____
_____
_____
_____

_____

_____

NEW DAY – NEW TIME

I ended the book talking about BOAZ, well in 2008 we married, after going through the marriage counseling, planning the wedding, him talking about needing to go talk with his deceased wife to tell her.

It's 2008 and we are getting married, close family and friends are at his moms for the ceremony. It was very nice; my great-aunt Dorothy was there and that meant so much to me. Other family was there also, but it's so interesting how when you are in a bad place family will seem to be all for you. The minute God lifts you up and things change for the better for you then they change, oh no, now they can't look at being in a better place than you are, you now are doing as well as they are. Actions and speech changes, you have gone be able to tell yourself, often, "don't take it personal".

We decided to go to a new church, as he did not want to go to my church since I was so involved there. We tried his church, but the first lady of the church was mad that he didn't marry her best friend and she made church miserable for me. She had the other women in the church showing me their Monday thru Saturday "Christian" side, glad I wasn't a "new Christian" as I might have changed my mind about church and Christianity. We finally agreed upon a church where no one knew either of us, again a man of God, who truly started using his FREE WILL. He was becoming a "Sunday only Christian" more and more.

A year later, it's our first anniversary, and my husband has gone from BOAZ to SAUL. By this time, he has learned that where I was when we met, was not "who" I was. He has learned that the circles he was in, I too had been in those same circles. Where he thought he was introducing me to, I had been a part of much more, entrepreneur, president of organizations, fundraiser, trainer. By our first-year anniversary his demeanor had changed. I was seeing another person, he begins being verbally abusive, he said things to me and my daughter to kick out self-esteem. In talking to one of his sisters I learned that his last two wives and the last girl friend were women with low self-esteems, well he had the right one this time. My mother kicked my self-esteem all through my living with her, I promised myself when I left her house no one would ever talk to me like that, I didn't need it. So, when he came at me, I went at him. When he took me to a board meeting, he was a part of, two of the people on the board knew me and told him you are marrying up, don't hurt her (before we were married). He could have been a powerful man of God in the places he would be going into, but his FREE WILL took it to another place.

POLITICS – WHAAAAAAAAAT?

We are invited to a meeting one day by a lady who is very strong in the political ring in Jacksonville, FL. She was looking for someone to chair a group that was being started and her eye was on my husband. The meeting went well, and he agreed to go under her wing to learn politics and what was going on in the political ring. So, he has received his 1st "title" and he now sees this title as a gateway to more, and he gets worse at home.

The more involved we get, the worse he gets "at home". He also has a problem with me making my own way in the political ring. Being from DC and having been a part of some things there, it was refreshing for me to have this new outlet for myself. We are going to all sorts of meetings after a while, meeting people and learning what is going on in our city as well as in our state.

A NEW COPYRIGHT – FOR TRAINING

I was called by someone in the city and asked if I could give them a price and courses for a janitorial program. I was contacted because my commercial company had done very well, until I shut it down, always thinking in the back of my mind to reopen it when the "time was right".

I create this program with God's help, my program is teaching the proper techniques of cleaning. I give this information to this person and don't think any more about it, this was late 2007. In April 2008 I get a phone call from this person, and I am asked if I would teach this program. When I told my husband, he said yes, I should teach it since I created it. So, I go in believing, my cleaning company is being contracted to provide this training, but a year later, after teaching and graduating the first class, I was asked to come on as an employee. I took the position in August and was told I would be paid one thing but was paid less. I stayed because I was providing this training to homeless veterans and ex-offenders, as this was the population God had me hiring and working with who worked with me. My commercial cleaning specialized in construction final cleaning, but in 2006 construction was going through issues with supplies, sheet rock was in high demand but short, etc.

I am starting to receive attention for the program and the graduates who are obtaining employment, you would think this would be a good thing, because it wasn't just about me, it was giving the program and the shelter attention. I am starting to see, when you "want" to make a difference for others, there are those whose nerves you will get on because their "talk of making a difference" is just that, only talk. I never thought I would get myself in trouble helping people. I began to notice that some people want to help from their heart, some people only help for the attention, and some people help for a cost. Hmmmmmmmmmmmmmmmmmm.

Time is marching on, the verbal abuse gets worse, I keep telling myself to honor my vows, keep being me, let him see God in me and he will stop. Well watching him with his mother and sisters, I began to see he kicks their self esteem also and they just go with it. I was not, I bucked at times, because I was not going to let him make my daughter feel like she was not worthy and didn't count. The more she and I did that he wasn't used to seeing the women in his life do and accomplish, the way we talked about ideas and goals and not people and stuff, he got worse.

HELPING WITH CAMPAIGNS

The more involved we became with the political party, the more we did, the more we began to live politics. My daughter even became a part of the teens in our political party, being Black in the party, showed me there were many of us in this ring, working people like us who wanted to help make a difference.

We worked on a presidential campaign and I learned a lot and saw that there are still those who don't want us to be a part but need us, WOW. Eye opener made me see that all through time, politics has always been about Blacks votes and money, we spend more money than any other race in the US.

It is now 2010 and we are working on the campaign for the governor of the state. It's exciting and interesting. We are in meetings, going around the state, following the candidate and helping where we can. The candidate wins and we are now frequenting the governor's mansion as invitees. I am seeing how God has made me no respecter of persons, as I was able to enjoy being with my students at the shelter during the day and then change and prepare for an evening at the governor's mansion or a conference in Orlando at the Gaylord. You must remain humble and let God lift you up and not man, you go much farther with God lifting you. Man will change, they can go from friend to enemy, from associate to stranger, from disliking you to hating you, God stays the same "ALWAYS".

GOD RELEASED ME

In 2011 God released me from my husband, as I
kept praying, reminding Him of his word that peace
and grace is how we are supposed to live, and I had
neither in our household. I kept saying all I want is
peace of mind and an air mattress (be careful what

you ask for, you must be specific   ).

April 2011, I got my peace of mind and an air
mattress, and I was in heaven. I separated from
him, I told him not to call, write, email, or text me.
Thirty days later, I get a call from him and he asked
me if I would still be secretary for our political
group, I told him I had to think about it and would
let him know and hung up. The Holy Spirit spoke
to me and said yes, do it, as he is going to lift you
up, unbeknown to himself. I didn't understand and
said ok.

So, I am ending this book, once again. I have to
say, I had no new allies, I feel like I'm out on a limb
alone, God is there, I feel Him from time to time. I
have to say thank you to God for helping me keep
my sanity in it all. Thanking Him for the
opportunities afforded me, even though there were
some who didn't want me to be in places I was in or
be a part of things I was a part of. What I learned
was I may help people and give my all, but I am not
to depend on them to do and be the same for me.
When you make the decision to "really" walk with
God and let Him guide you, it can be lonely, you
crazy a lot of times, and people will look at you and

talk about you wondering what in hell you are doing. God takes you out of the "normal" and have you moving in what looks like impossible to those on the outside looking in.

To those on their walk and in their journey letting God totally lead, you are not alone, ask God to lead you to that someone who you can talk to and not feel strange, because they are going through their own thing.

My next book, which will take you through the rest of the journey, a lot happened. But I can now tell the story without any animosity, disdain, and more. I can tell what happened in a way that allows me to release and relate. So, I will see you in the next book, "RIZ3 LIK3 A PHOENIX".

This book has been edited into a new edition with new information. Take care and thank you for buying my book, I hope you enjoyed it.

www.ingramcontent.com/pod-product-compliance
Lightning Source LLC
Chambersburg PA
CBHW051811040426
42446CB00007B/613

* 9 7 9 8 9 9 9 1 5 5 3 9 0 2 *